Discovering Another Way

Discovering
Another Way

*Raising Brighter Children
While Having a Meaningful Career*

LANE NEMETH

BEYOND
WORDS
Publishing
I N C

Beyond Words Publishing, Inc.

20827 N.W. Cornell Road, Suite 500

Hillsboro, Oregon 97124-9808

503-531-8700   1-800-284-9673

Cover/interior design and composition: Susan Shankin

Managing editor: Kathy Matthews

Proofreader: Marvin Moore

Printed in the United States of America

Distributed to the book trade by Publishers Group West

Library of Congress Cataloging-in-Publication Data

Nemeth, Lane.

  Discovering another way : raising brighter children while having a meaningful career / Lane Nemeth.

    p. cm.

  ISBN 1-58270-010-9 (pbk.)

  1. Discovery Toys, Inc. 2. Nemeth, Lane. 3. Toy industry—United States.
4. Businesswomen—United States Biography. 5. Entrepreneurship—United States Case studies. 6. Women-owned business enterprises—United States Case studies.
7. Small business—United States—Management Case studies. I. Title.

HD9993.T694D576   1999

338.7'68872'092—dc21

  [B]   99-32776

                                                                              CIP

The corporate mission of Beyond Words Publishing, Inc.:

Inspire to Integrity

*To my beloved husband, who has put up with the rigors
of having a driven, entrepreneurial wife and has never faltered in
his love and support. And to the reason my life is continuously
filled with sunshine and delight, my daughter, Tara.
And finally, to my ever so special parents, who by bringing me
up with nonjudgmental love, integrity, and wisdom
allowed me to become a driven, entrepreneurial wife!*

Contents

Prologue

I AM WAITING IN THE DARK, behind a curtain. I listen silently as a children's dance troupe performs. I'm attuned to the laughter, excitement, and applause of an audience I can't see, and I'm as enraptured as that unseen audience while images of the rehearsals I've watched previously unwind in my head. I can tell by the music that their performance is coming to an end—which means that mine must soon begin.

My legs are shaking and my stomach is churning; in a few moments I must walk out and face almost three thousand women, all of whom are part of the company I founded, Discovery Toys, Inc. Why am I always convinced that I will step out on the stage and not remember one single word I want to say?

Three thousand people filling every seat in the hall! I flash back to my first convention, in Benicia, California, which every single Educational Consultant in the company attended—all thirty of them! I can't really comprehend how far we've come in a few short years.

A warm August morning has dawned on the opening session of our annual convention, and I am about to give the keynote address. Discovery Toys, Inc., now has annual revenues just under $100 million. We sell the highest-quality fun, educational, and developmental toys available. We've won numerous awards for many of the toys we developed ourselves. We've reached hundreds of thousands of families with our unique toys and games. Now we are introducing books and software from our new Discovery Quest division. Thousands of women across the country sell our products, but they all work for themselves, setting their own hours and income goals.

My company and I have come a long way since July 1977, when a UPS truck delivered the first few boxes of carefully chosen educational toys to my garage—boxes that were soon to overflow into the kitchen, bathroom, and bedrooms. Three other women and I took those toys to friends' houses, where we showed other parents how educational toys are an essential part of good parenting. From my one-car garage, we have grown to a 180,000-square-foot warehouse. From our first three pioneers, we have grown to the thirty thousand Educational Consultants, whom we call ECs, who proudly sell our products today.

The show's producer, David Goff, approaches me with a hand-held mike and whispers that Janice Mazibrook, my vice president of sales, is approaching the podium. She will be thanking the children, welcoming our guests, and beginning my introduction.

Suddenly I'm having trouble breathing. When I walk out to center stage, I won't be able to see any faces; the spotlights will glare in my eyes, making the audience invisible. I'll only be able to hear them. The talented children who have just performed are a tough act to follow.

Besides trembling legs and a churning stomach, there is something else beginning to happen to me. As I listen to the enthusiastic audience cheer the talented children, I become elated. Sitting out there are thousands of successful women. Some of them are earning a hundred dollars, some hundreds of thousands of dollars. The variations in income, lifestyle, families, and geography are endless. The similarities exist in our desire to be recognized, to have work we know brings happiness and value to other families, to earn as much money as we individually deem important, and to enjoy the support of other women like ourselves. But the biggest driver is that we won't allow a boss to tell us when we can be with our children.

These women have all chosen to design their own careers while keeping family first. Discovery Toys is a great option. But there are literally endless options available to you. We all have talents and opportunities. Helping you to discover and use your unique talents is the reason I felt compelled to write this book. Allow yourself the freedom to dream, and your dream can lead you to freedom.

1. The Great Dilemma

AS A NEW MOTHER, I was confronted by a dilemma that may be familiar to some readers: I was devoted to my child and going crazy at the same time. Over the past twenty years, in my personal and professional life, I have talked to thousands of mothers. Some have chosen to be stay-at-home moms, while some have chosen—or have felt the need—to work full time.

Do you know what I discovered? Each side looks enviously at the other. The stay-at-homes envy the working moms because the latter have adult stimulation and earn money, which not only buys things but which balances power at home. The working moms envy the stay-at-homes—sometimes desperately—because they have time with their kids.

Each side also has some things to be happy about. Stay-at-home moms feel lucky to have that time with their children—to take them to doctor appointments, to read to them, and just to watch them grow. But many are isolated, living out in the suburbs, with extended family nonexistent or far away. And as much as they love their children, they long for recognition for something other than getting their husband's undershirts their whitest-white. They look around and think, "There must be another way."

Working moms often love their careers, their co-workers, and of course, their added income. They like having somewhere to go in something nicer than sweatshirts and jeans. But they know what every working mom finds out soon enough: ***The balancing act is a myth.*** They're tired, they don't have enough time for their kids or their husbands, and time for themselves isn't even on the waiting list. They look around and think, "There must be another way."

I know. At different times, I've been both a stay-at-home mom and a working mom. When I stayed at home, I wondered what was wrong with me and why I was starting to go crazy around noon. And when I worked, I secretly believed that other women had the balancing act down and never felt guilty or tired or stressed.

For me, the answer lay in working part time. And for thousands of women over the years, Discovery Toys has provided the opportunity to work part time or full time from home, allowing them to be available for their families while still having adult stimulation and extra income.

I believe that working part time from home is an excellent way to resolve the conflict between the craziness of staying at home and the inordinate pressure of working full time. But every woman has to find her own way. I hope that by sharing my story I can help you find your way.

❏   ❑   ❏

I believe that each of us has a calling, a unique gift that we can contribute to the world. My gifts lie in being an entrepreneur, a creative educator, and most importantly, a mother. I wrote this book to help you discover your own gifts. Perhaps you too can use them in a totally new way to create for yourself a lucrative, part-time career that will enable you to be personally satisfied and that at the same time will let you keep your family first.

From early on, I knew that I cared about children and wanted to serve them, to make the world a safer, more nurturing place for them to live. I've had many jobs, but it was my interest in children that led me to earn a master's degree in education and eventually to become the director of a large, state-funded day-care center.

I didn't consciously aspire to more. But I was restless, and when I saw an opportunity to combine entrepreneurism with empowering children and women, I jumped at it. And so Discovery Toys was born.

I had become a parent at the age of twenty-nine. I wanted to bring everything I knew about education to my own daughter's childhood so that she would grow up smart and confident—and it was my desire to get her the best possible toys that led in large part to the business I birthed.

As a parent, my formal background paid off, and you will note, perhaps, an interesting contrast between my naïveté in the business world and my own confidence at home.

That contrast is at the core of this book. One myth about creativity is that it flourishes only in an atmosphere of calm. Calm can be very nice—but the truth is that some of our most beneficial insights come at times when we are most pressed, most torn between work and family, most challenged by our own inexperience. If we are willing to live the contradictions, willing to exist in a state of tension and to confront it, then we can truly grow.

These times when stress and contradiction lead to revelation are what I call "Learning Moments." In a Learning Moment, a person expands his or her capacity by acquiring new skills, insight, or knowledge. But Learning Moments are not confined to periods of stress and contradiction; as we'll see, they come in a wide variety of shapes and sizes.

Throughout this book, I have identified some of the Learning Moments that occurred for me while I struggled with work and family.

These Learning Moments have been identified with a variety of symbols:

 for Learning Moments of insight.

 for Learning Moments of the heart.

 for Learning Moments related to business.

 for Learning Moments connected to balancing our lives.

 for Learning Moments about family.

 for Learning Moments that help us recognize those special people who intervene on our behalf for reasons other than personal gain.

I wish that there could actually be someone to tap all of us on the shoulder and tell us that we've just had a Learning Moment. In fact, sometimes it does happen that way, but more often it takes anywhere from a few days to a few years—and sometimes a dollop of psychotherapy—to recognize our Learning Moments. My hope is that by reading about mine, you will become more in tune with your own as they occur.

I've been a wife and mother as well as an educator and businesswoman. So, along with pointing out Learning Moments, I've distilled some of what I've learned into a number of sections that target relevant areas of parenting, marriage, and career.

❑   ❑   ❑

Learning Moments begin at birth. We're born with all the brain cells we need to get through life, and if we're lucky enough to have the right stimulation at the right time, then we can use our brains to their fullest potential. It's our responsibility as parents to ensure that our children have all the tools they need to create their own Learning Moments. Those tools include appropriate toys, books, games, and—by far the most important—playtime with and attention from their parents. (See chapter 2, "Learning Moments.")

I founded Discovery Toys because I wanted to help raise a generation of smarter kids; I have always seen Discovery Toys not as a toy company but as a parenting company, and this book, I hope, will be part of my longtime mission, which started back in the early '70s when I was a preschool teacher, to help parents to parent. I also desperately wanted to find a way to help women earn as much money as they wished while still being able to maintain their families as their top priority. There are many sections in this book about starting your own home-based business by using your skills and talents or about simply reexamining your income to see if you really can stay at home with your children if you wish to.

❏ ❏ ❏

If a child learns to learn in her first years, she develops a lifelong capacity. You can see my capacity borne out in my story, because although I made many, many mistakes, I managed to learn from them rather than let them permanently sidetrack me from my goal. Thanks to my Learning Moments, Discovery Toys is alive and well and thriving; it has brought joy to millions of children over the years.

2. Learning Moments

D AVID, A FRIEND OF MINE, recently got a job teaching a class on the history of the theater at a local private university. David is both brilliant and dedicated, and he was up late many an evening crafting his lectures. As weeks went by, he was often discouraged to see his students fidgeting or doodling during those lectures, and he noticed that there were few questions when he discussed the plays he had assigned.

The week before the midterm, several students approached him: "Aren't you going to give us a study guide? The other profs do."

What the students wanted, it turned out, was a list of facts to memorize for the test. Few had read any of the assigned material. David was appalled. "You don't learn anything that way," he said. "You're memorizing without understanding. In the long run, you'll forget it all and it will be as if you never took this class."

His students didn't care. They cared about what letter grade they got—what would appear on their transcript when graduate schools or employers looked at it.

The parents of these young adults had not helped them make Learning Moments for themselves when they were children.

Children have an inborn desire to explore the world around them. An infant expresses that desire when he puts his rattle in his mouth; he's exploring its size, taste, and texture. Later, when he's a toddler, you see him fill containers and dump them out, exploring spatial relationships. Similarly, when he plays with blocks, he is learning about balance and practicing the hand-eye coordination that is a prerequisite for reading and writing. But he doesn't know that—he only knows that he has built an impressive tower.

My philosophy is that we as parents should stand behind our children, not in front of them. Let them lead the way. Observe your child. What is she trying to do? What do you think she might be trying to discover? How can you give her the tools and create an environment to facilitate that discovery? If she likes to bang on pots and pans to hear the sounds they make, can you give her other music-making—or even just noise-making—tools? If she likes to put play-dough together to form different shapes, can you find toys or other baby-safe household items that she can combine and recombine? In other words, encourage her natural inclinations.

Rather than imposing your own standards about learning on your child, this approach will give her the greatest opportunity to learn for herself. You might be tempted to ask yourself, "Susie down the street is reading, and she's only four. Why isn't my son Bobbie reading, too?" Accept that children grow and develop in their own way and in their own time. In fact, most children do not read comfortably, and some not at all, until the age of eight. The reality is that the child who learns at four and the child who learns at eight, all else being equal, will be at the same grade level by the time they are nine. Of course, encouraging your child to learn is commendable! But pushing them to do something before they are ready is not only an exercise in futility but can be damaging as well.

The child who progresses in her own way and in her own time from making a square out of two play-dough triangles to doing geometry not only will master geometry but will take pride in her mastery of the subject. To get there, she needs both freedom to experiment with the world around her as well as your guidance to keep her out of trouble.

❏   ❏   ❏

Opportunities for Learning Moments exist throughout the most ordinary of days. Merely by being aware of these opportunities, you can start to take advantage of them.

You will also discover many more learning opportunities if you are able to make an essential paradigm shift, a fundamental change in the way you look at your child. When a baby drops food off the tray of his high chair or throws it from the stroller, he's not trying to make a mess for you to clean up—he wants to see what will happen when the food drops! He's learning about spatial relationships, about cause and effect, about object constancy. (If the bottle disappears behind the stroller, does it still exist?) You don't have to whistle a merry tune while you clean up, but you can accommodate his thinking and turn a negative into a positive. When he drops the bath towel into the tub you just filled, you can find out together how much water it absorbed. While you're at it, try dropping a sponge and a washcloth along with the towel and compare the absorbing powers of all three!

Along this line, remember that "mistakes" do not exist in Learning Moments. If your child draws a three-legged dog, don't correct him; comment on his inventiveness.

Here are some more suggestions:

❏ Take your toddler or preschooler on a walk. Go to the woods or just stroll through your neighborhood park and explore. Babies love textures, colors, and sounds. Listen to birds; follow a caterpillar; feel the barks of different trees and comment on the different textures; look at the leaves and compare their varied patterns and shades of green.

❑ Make music. Get out pots and pans, some plastic containers, and a wooden spoon, and let your two-year-old bang away. While she's banging, simply comment on the different sounds she's making.

❑ Provide child-sized tools: cooking utensils, cups, and silverware that fit small hands. Get your child a small table and chair.

❑ Always have art supplies available at home: paper, pens, paints, and glue. Starting as early as twelve months, kids love and need to express themselves visually. Don't limit their projects by trying to keep them neat; I think newspaper was invented primarily to put under kids' artwork. Kids love to glue bits of paper to paper plates or to Styrofoam meat trays; they love to work with glitter, sequins, and feathers. "Found art" can be inexpensive; let them use old buttons, pebbles, or leaves in their projects. Coloring books have their place, but they present a model for a child and are likely to inhibit their creativity.

Another great idea is to supply kids with butcher paper—long rolls of wide paper that you can purchase at arts-and-crafts stores. Why confine them to the limitations of a measly 8½-by-11-inch piece of paper? Let them keep unrolling the paper and see where it leads. Have them lie down on the paper; you can trace the outline of their bodies, arms, and legs spread out, and then they can draw in their own faces and clothes—or whatever they want.

❑ Don't judge. When your child shows you her artwork, try to resist the temptation to tell her that it's good. "Good" is a judgment, and art is too personal to judge. Comment instead on the content—the colors, the shapes, the materials.

Ask her to tell you about what's going on in her painting, what she felt when she was painting it, what she wanted to communicate.

❑ Let your kids play dress-up. Three- to six-year-olds particularly love this, boys as well as girls. You don't need to spend money on fancy costume sets—just dig into your closet and use your imagination. Old scarves, costume jewelry, and nightgowns have unlimited possibilities. I know a little girl who turned her mother's half-slip into a veil and a tablecloth into a bridal train.

❑ The supermarket is a veritable university. For a younger child, there are colors and shapes to identify, fruits and vegetables and other foods to name. Send an older child to get three carrots and two cucumbers, then let her tell you how many vegetables she has altogether.

You can also play "shopping" at home. Act as the cashier and let your child bring you various items from around the house. Tell her what they cost and let her pay you with play money. (Making money out of colored paper can be another project, or you can use money from a Monopoly or other board game.) This can be a counting game when you count out bills, an addition game when you come up with a total, and a subtraction game when you give change.

❑ Laundry, dishes, and other household items provide opportunities for toddlers to practice sorting and matching.

❑ Keep one or more kid-friendly encyclopedias at home. If your child asks you, "When do ants sleep?" you can go look it up together.

Increasingly, people look to on-line encyclopedias for information, and these certainly can play a valuable role in our lives. But I believe strongly in the old-fashioned, bound kind for a couple of reasons. First, they're more portable. That makes them more fun for you and your child to share. You can cuddle up on the couch and read them together or take them into the backyard.

Second, bound encyclopedias are right there. The essence of a Learning Moment is its immediacy. As fast as computers have become, even the time it takes to boot one up and load the right software can mean that you postpone looking for the answer—and the moment is lost.

Third, bound encyclopedias invite continued exploration in a way that electronic ones do not. If you do a search on "turtles," you will get a screen full of information on turtles, which is fine but closed-ended. If you look up "turtles" in a bound encyclopedia, soon you'll be flipping pages and browsing through "turnstiles" and "twilight."

❐   ❑   ❐

Your child's most important teacher is you, so you bear an enormous responsibility. However much we may need to improve education in this country, we cannot shift that primary responsibility to others. The good news is that by creating Learning Moments, by being a role model, and by using some of the parenting techniques we'll discuss in this book, you can fulfill that responsibility to your child and bring him up filled with wonder at the world that surrounds him.

3. Decisions, Decisions

L AX—LOS ANGELES INTERNATIONAL—is not the world's most
intimidating airport, it's only one of them. And Friday morning is
not the craziest time of the week there, just almost.

I was on a United flight from San Francisco. With me was my
friend and mentor, Sue Nurock, a professor of early childhood education who was a large, maternal woman with long, graying hair and a
warm smile. We had met, of all places, in the bathroom at a community college in Northern California.

Our plane hit the runway with a thud; the engines went into
reverse. I gripped the arm of my seat. "Scared?" Sue asked.

"Not of flying," I replied through gritted teeth.

In 1977, I was thirty years old, a new mother, and also the director of the Concord Child Care Center. At the day-care center we had
plenty of child-friendly, educational toys, books, and games that the
kids loved. I personally ordered these toys from specialty catalogs of
companies that supplied schools and day-care centers such as ours.

But I had discovered that I couldn't buy those same kinds of toys
for my own two-year-old daughter. Being the obsessive mother of one
child, I was determined to give her only the very best of everything.

Since I knew firsthand what a huge difference the right educational/developmental products have on children, she wasn't going to get any "junk toys" from me! She was going to have playthings that not only were great fun but that also were stimulating and developmental and would give her a big head start in the world.

Why shouldn't the general public—and I—be able to buy the same toys and games that we used at the day-care center? It seemed a pretty simple problem to solve, and I had decided that I was the person to solve it. I wanted to start an educational toy company and revolutionize the toy industry.

That's why I was landing in Los Angeles. I loosened my grip on the armrest as the plane slowed, taxiing toward the terminal, while Sue in the window seat gazed out across the field.

My idea of exactly how I was going start an educational toy company and revolutionize the toy industry was as vague as my desire was intense. But perhaps I was blessed by my naïveté. I had heard about a toy trade show in L.A., and Sue and I had decided to check it out. I was thrilled that I had been able to talk Sue into coming along; she thought it would be great fun, while I was terrified.

I had borrowed money from my grandmother to buy the plane tickets. Sue and I were schoolteachers with solid backgrounds in education who loved kids—and were absolutely clueless about business.

I hoped to learn something about how the industry worked: who the various toy manufacturers were, which toys they made, and how I could buy them. Since the toy show was for retailers, in order to get in we had spent $25 on business cards that had "The Learning Place" and our names printed on them.

We walked off the jetway to join the madness of a weekend about to begin—tourists, businesspeople, and college kids arriving and departing. I grew up in New York City, so I was hardly frightened by crowds. But somehow, as Sue and I plodded down corridors, rode escalators, and jostled among other travelers on our long journey to baggage claim, the whole atmosphere added to my growing suspicion that I was in way over my head. Who was I to think about starting a business? The sum total of my sales experience was selling tickets to the annual raffle at my high school. I had barely balanced my checkbook for the last five years.

Our fear of failure can block our success before we begin.

And then we were at baggage claim, surrounded by the beautiful people of L.A. Even the skycaps were splendid. Someone once explained this phenomenon to me: every year, the single most gorgeous young man and young woman from every high school in the nation comes to Hollywood to become a star. A very few of them do become famous, and many of those who don't go home. But the rest simply stay in L.A., where their day job becomes their career. And so, even at the airport, you will see a stunning blonde behind the car-rental counter, a tall man with chiseled features emptying the trash.

Once Sue and I had our suitcases, we dragged them over to the corner where local hotels and motels displayed large signs next to phones that would let us dial them directly.

"We should have gotten a place to stay before we came down here," Sue mumbled, surveying our options.

Of course we should have. Standing with my battered duffle bag in front of a picture of the Bonaventure Hotel, it hit me full force that I hadn't even made a reservation for the weekend. Everything was going to be sold out. We'd end up on a bench in Griffith Park. What in God's name was I thinking?

I opened my mouth with every intention of saying, "Let's go home." Why not? I would lose nothing but the cost of my ticket. Home was my comfortable bed, my supportive husband, my beloved two-year-old daughter. Los Angeles was noise and crowds and nowhere to go and $25 business cards that suddenly seemed phony.

"What's wrong?" Sue asked. Then she added, "Don't worry, we'll find a place to stay."

"I know," I murmured. "It's just—." A woman with a double stroller bumped into me from behind.

"Excuse me," she said, and went on.

"It's just . . ." I tried again. But I couldn't put it into words, not then. I can today. It was the Discovery Toys mission. I had seen what was out there—GI Joe with his camouflage and war paraphernalia and Barbie with her total emphasis on the perfect face and figure and fancy gowns and minuscule stiletto heels. I knew I could do better. It was then that I developed my personal mission statement. I wanted—I still want—to bring quality toys to children, toys that not only entertain but that help those children to grow up smarter and more confident, while giving women more choices about how they raise their children. Everything I've done since that point is held up to this vision.

Recognize your mission, and your passion will drive you.

Even without explicitly being put into words, that mission was inside of me, and it kept me from returning home. "You're right," was all I said. "Let's see if the Biltmore has any more rooms. We can just about afford it."

4. To Work or Not to Work

MOVE THE CLOCK BACK a year and a half. I was sitting on the floor of my tiny rented house in Concord, California. Concord is an unpretentious bedroom community where my husband, Ed, and I had lived since moving to the San Francisco Bay area two years before.

On the floor with me was my six-month-old daughter, Tara. She had two teeth jutting from the center of her lower gums, and she was so proud of the fact that she could sit up all by herself. She was the absolute love of my life.

She was alternately shaking a rattle and putting it in her mouth. Her feet were bare; the soles were pink and perfect. Her toes were tiny miracles.

I had worshipped this baby since the moment that the doctor put all eight pounds, eight ounces of her on my chest. I wanted the very best for her, and I knew that she would be my first thought until the moment I die.

But as we played peek-a-boo, I was thinking about going back to work part time.

When Tara was born, I had taken a six-month maternity leave, even though I had no intention of going back to work—for myself as much as for her. And to do what no one else could do: to make our parent/child bond as strong as possible.

Actually, I never seriously considered any other alternative. My own mother had stayed home to raise her two daughters. In 1975, when Tara was born, Mom staying home with her kids was still the norm, although that was beginning to change. But to my way of thinking, the financial sacrifice was unimportant compared with being Tara's mom. That was priceless.

After six months, I was facing a crisis. To put it another way, I was going crazy. My adoration of Tara had only increased, which I wouldn't have thought possible, as she grew and revealed her curious, playful nature. But I had to face up to what was going on for me. The relentless needs of infants and toddlers affect different people in different ways. Tara would fall sleep only if she were in my arms, and around noon of our long days together—my husband, Ed, often didn't get home until eight at night—I was transformed into a person whom I wouldn't want taking care of my daughter. I'd start thinking, When, oh when, is she going to take a real nap? Finally she'd drift off to sleep, giving me a much-needed break and restoring my emotional balance. But the fact was that I was still often tense and irritable. I would long to get out of the house—alone.

I was shocked that this was happening, and that realization was accompanied by a 7.1 tremor of guilt. What was wrong with me? I could deal with preschoolers for hours without a murmur. But this was my own daughter!

I believe that many women struggle with the same conflict between what they think should be and what is. Even today we are so inundated with images of the perfectly calm, perfectly happy mother sitting in a rocking chair humming to her sleeping infant—of course the infant is always asleep!—that we regard anything short of that ideal with suspicion.

You're not alone in your dilemma. Many women are torn between work and family.

You have a baby. Suddenly you can't go to the mailbox without packing a diaper bag. You're losing touch with your friends who don't have children. You can't even keep up with the news because the baby continually tries to put the paper in her mouth. But to complain would somehow imply that you aren't in love with your child, which you of course are.

That day, sitting on the floor with Tara, I confronted this issue, and I decided to go back to work, just for a few hours in the afternoon, at the day-care center. It may seem like a casual decision, but for me it was gut-wrenching—as I believe it is for many women, who are not allowed to admit it, especially to themselves.

Working in the childcare profession, I had one advantage, at least: I had connections to some special people. I was able to hire a gifted young woman, Laura, who taught at the center in the mornings and who was interested in working afternoons as well, to come to the house and be with Tara one-on-one for a few hours a day. (See chapter 15, "Childcare Options.")

It was a great idea—until the day I left for the first time. Tara and I had not yet been apart during her short life. The pain and guilt were staggering. How could I desert my six-month-old daughter, the baby I'd longed eight years for? What if the house burned down? What if Laura, trusted friend and teacher, actually had a multiple-personality disorder and I had simply not yet become acquainted with Alternate Self Number 16, Brunehilde the Child Abuser?

At this juncture in my life I had two choices: to continue with the way I believed I was supposed to live, being miserable every afternoon and confusing my daughter when I lost my patience from simple exhaustion, or to make a change. I am proud that I was able to be honest enough with myself to see that I needed to make this change.

Learn to be honest with yourself about your needs.

Somehow, I dragged myself out of the house. When I returned home at 5:15 P.M. after working part time for the first time since Tara was born, I was terrified that she wouldn't even look at me. Perhaps I had broken a sacred trust and she would hate me forever.

Instead, she fell into my arms giggling and started to nurse. Clearly, she was doing better than I was.

Sometimes we project our own needs and fears onto our children.

She soon developed a secure bond with Laura. After her long nap—why not? there was no Mommy at home to torture!—they played games and had tons of fun. By the time I walked in the door again around five, I couldn't wait to spend the rest of the evening with her.

Sure, change is almost always terrifying. But this change, as so often happens, turned out to be beneficial for everyone. Because we had those few hours apart, I always looked forward to the time I had with Tara. I planned my work around her schedule. When we were together, which was still most of her waking day, I focused entirely on her. I had promised myself when Tara was born that I would never raise my voice to her. And largely because I have also nurtured myself with the outside stimulation I needed, I have been able to keep that promise for twenty-three years.

◻ ◻ ◻

When I look back on my life, many moments, many decisions, stand out. Here are two, but they were significant: my decision to move forward with Discovery Toys, and my decision to go back to work part time—thus laying the foundation for Discovery Toys. Later I will share others with you.

What decisions stand out for you? You had a chance to go away to college, but it meant taking the risk of leaving your family. You were offered a new job, but you weren't sure your skills were up to it. You wanted a baby, but you weren't sure what kind of parent you would be. What did you do? Do we live our lives in constant fear or acknowledge our fear and move forward anyway?

In a small way, these decisions confront us every day. What will you have for lunch? It could be a fast-food hamburger or a healthy salad. What will you say to your children when they come home from school? You could sit down and talk to them about their day or send them into the living room to watch television.

Big or small, day after day, these decisions make up a life—potentially, a life of health and well-being, a life of communication and closeness, a life of challenge and reward.

I've been blessed by a lot of luck over the years. But ultimately, if I've been successful, it's also because I've often been able to push myself beyond my comfort zone, take a chance, and do what was unfamiliar. There is no question that you can as well.

TO MY GROWN-UP CHILD

My life was busy through the day
I didn't have much time to play
The little games you asked me to.
I didn't have much time for you
I'd go to work, come home and cook,
But when you'd bring your picture book
And ask me please to share your fun
I'd say: "A little later, hon"
I'd tuck you in all safe at night,
And hear your prayers, turn out the light,
Then tiptoe softly to the door—
I wish I'd stayed a minute more.
For life is short, the years rush past—
A little child grows up so fast.
No longer standing at your side
With precious secrets to confide
The picture books are put away,
There are no longer games to play
No goodnight kiss, no prayers to hear—
That all belongs to yesteryear.
My hands, once busy, now are still
The days are long and hard to fill
I wish I could go back and do
The little things you asked me to.

AUTHOR UNKNOWN

5. What Do You Mean, I Can't Buy These Toys?

THERE WERE ABOUT sixty children in the Concord Child Care Center, ranging from two to ten years old. I was the director of the center, running the show and loving it. I had a staff of about fifteen people, some full time and some part time, all professional, all dedicated.

In 1976, the women's movement of the late '60s—the daring pronouncements of Gloria Steinem and Betty Friedan—was finally translating into numbers, and some women were going back to work. To what extent women really had more choices and to what extent that choice was an illusion—was and still is—is another story. But meanwhile, at the Concord Center, we were doing a good job of caring for children while their mothers were working.

In fact, I was one of those moms myself. I've already described how I decided to go back to work part time when Tara was six months old. I had somehow convinced the board of directors that I would be a better director for the center part time than anyone they could find full time.

I had always cared deeply about children, long before I became a mother myself. I'd already received a master's degree in education and had previously worked in childcare.

An incident occurred during my tenure in Concord that fueled my passion further. I began to have suspicions about a little girl who was attending the center. She said odd things that led me to fear that she was being sexually abused by her father. When I asked her where her mother was, her replies were vague and uncertain.

I contacted several agencies about my concern, but they said they could do nothing. I had one last recourse: The little girl had a British accent, so I contacted Interpol, the international police organization.

My hunch was correct. The girl had been kidnapped from her mother in London. When the mother arrived to reclaim her child, we had a celebration like you've never seen. My part in this reunion remains one of my proudest achievements.

At the same time, I remained shaken for many months. The idea that someone could treat a child this way—smuggling her across the border like contraband in the lining of a suitcase—was nearly more than I could handle. Was this what children could expect from the world? I prayed not, and I prayed that I could be a part of making it better.

And working with these children day-to-day, I began to see the undramatic but enormously important way in which I could make things better. Children's hearts and minds are like fertile soil. The seeds of positive adult attention easily take root and flower. I watched little ones play with our fabulous developmental toys, books, and games. I watched them do things like master simple puzzles—a key pre-reading skill—and go on to more complex puzzles. I saw how their confidence grew step-by-step, and I was grateful for my part in contributing to this development.

❐   ❏   ❐

Being partly a creature of the government, the Concord Center had special advantages and problems. The cost to parents was low, and because of my relationship with Sue Nurock, the woman who went to L.A.

with me and who was a professor of early childhood education, we had extra hands: Sue would sometimes send us her students who needed supervised teaching hours, resulting in a high ratio of adults to kids, which is a necessity for good day care.

We had ample food, including surplus milk and cheese. We even had a cook! Perhaps best of all, we had a generous toy budget. But we were also subject to inevitable bureaucratic inanities. For example, we could buy virtually unlimited toys, books, games, and art supplies, as long as they were under $50 each. Anything over $50 was considered a "capital outlay" and therefore *verboten*. We raised money from local clubs like the Kiwanis in order to buy an outdoor shed in which to store those plentiful under-$50 toys.

The toys and games themselves were designated as educational and therefore were manufactured strictly for institutions like schools and day-care centers. It was my happy job to choose and purchase them from one of the educational catalogs. These catalogs were about as exciting as the white pages. The distributors had been marketing educational toys since the days of the one-room schoolhouse, and they displayed and described them just like so many school accessories—chalk or folding chairs. But the toys and games themselves were fabulous. They were sturdily fashioned to withstand the mauling of hundreds of small hands over many years. And they were truly educational. There were colorful wooden puzzles and blocks in graduated sizes and picture cards to put in sequence or to match and so many more. (See chapter 6, "Guidelines for Brain-Building Play.")

These playthings were correctly considered educational because of how crucial they are to a child's development. Take something as simple as stacking cups in different colors. A one-year-old uses them to build a tower. She's developing her fine motor coordination, her sense of spatial relationships, and in sizing them, pre-math skills. Take what looks like a simple matching game. A preschooler puts a picture of a zebra on top of another picture of a zebra. He's acquiring pre-reading skills by learning to discriminate among big pictures, which will lead to learning to discriminate between smaller pictures and eventually between *b*'s and *d*'s.

Today, some twenty years later, and thanks in large part to Discovery Toys, educational toys are more widely available—although manufacturers love to slap the word *educational* on almost everything. If you go into a specialty toy store, you will see some of these concepts applied to infant, toddler, and preschool toys, although often they're not as well-made. But in the mid-'70s, there were virtually no educational toys whatsoever to be found outside of institutions.

For the time being, though, I was blissfully unaware of the limitations of my local toy store, because I didn't need to go to the toy store. We had such stimulating toys at the day-care center that I got in the habit of borrowing them and taking them home on the weekend for Tara to play with.

I loved to watch her with these toys. I remember some special rattles that she particularly adored. They were lightweight, covered with different textures, and decorated with rudimentary human faces. (Later they inspired some of Discovery Toys' first rattles.) By contrast, a rattle that someone gave her from a toy store was so heavy that when she conked herself by accident she raised a welt on her forehead.

I knew, of course, that borrowing toys was taking unfair advantage of my position, and I didn't do it for long. Instead, I started ordering the toys I wanted when I ordered for the center, and I would immediately write the center a personal check when my products arrived.

It seemed like a perfectly logical arrangement. The center wasn't out a single penny, and Tara got the toys she loved. Except—silly me—I had forgotten that I was working for a government-sponsored program.

In late 1976, the Concord Child Care Center had its annual audit by the state Department of Education. Two men in gray pinstripe suits arrived with their narrow briefcases. They sat in my office for three hours, reviewing carefully typed spreadsheets. Everything was in order—except for one thing. What were these checks to the center from Lane Nemeth?

I explained.

"No, no, no," they said. "You can't do that."

"Why not?" I asked.

"There's no column. There's no place to write the checks from Lane Nemeth," they replied.

"You know I could have stolen those toys, and you never would have known. But I was honest, and now you are going to punish me when I've done nothing wrong?"

I'm one of those people who hates to be told "You can't do that"— especially when it makes absolutely no sense. On the other hand, I had been working with the state bureaucracy long enough to know that it wasn't worth a huge fight because it would never get me anywhere. So, with a big sigh, I promised the auditors that there would be no more checks from Lane Nemeth. But I was not about to have in my home, for Tara, anything less than the perfect products I taught with at school. I would have to find a way. I just didn't know what it would be—yet.

 Pick your battles at home and work carefully. Don't waste energy, for there's almost always another way to get what you need.

It was unfortunate timing, because I had been just about to buy a gift from one of those educational catalogs. A good friend of mine, Sheila Gutman, had a little boy, Kenny, who was exactly three months older than my daughter. Sheila's and my pregnancies had overlapped, and we had bonded over the joys and discomforts, from weight gain to leg cramps. Then, after our babies were born, we continued sharing the daily discoveries of new motherhood.

Kenny was about to celebrate his first birthday. I wanted to buy him something special. He was Sheila's son, and besides, I was an educator and the director of a day-care center. The pressure was on—granted that, as usual, the pressure was internal.

Since buying Kenny something from one of the catalogs was no longer an option, I went on a shopping trip to small stores in my neighborhood, to big stores in the mall, and to department stores.

And I couldn't find a thing I wanted to give him. I had something in my head, and nothing matched. For the first time I had to confront those oversized splashy boxes containing GI Joes and Barbies, board games that centered around unwieldy clowns, alligators that used four C batteries just to spit out balls, rattles that were boring and understimulating, and pull toys that fell over when pulled. I gave up. Disappointed, I settled on buying clothes for Kenny instead.

A shopping trip is a pretty common occurrence in the life of a mom. Even the state audit, while not something I did for fun, was an ordinary event. So it always seems funny to me now to look back and see how those two incidents, juxtaposed as they were, led to such a big change in my life—and, with all due modesty, in the whole toy industry.

Even ordinary events can be opportunities for big changes in your life.

The truth was that, at this point, I was looking to get away from the day-care center, even though I was proud of what we had accomplished. When I had joined a few years before, the center was housed in a deteriorating building that hadn't been painted since the Hoover administration. We literally had to stuff rags into the mouse holes. Together, my staff, the board, and I had raised money—remember, we had government funding for the things *they* thought were important—to move to a sparkling new facility with new unstop-upable toilets, a capacious refrigerator, and a beautiful backyard, complete with a huge wooden play structure and a real trike path.

Much more importantly, we were ahead of our time in our teaching methods. We had an open classroom with learning centers among which the children could move freely, and we had enough portable equipment for equally interesting activities outside to develop specific skills and muscles, along with free play. We had a curriculum with daily lesson plans as thorough as in any elementary school. I spent a lot of time explaining to those parents who were interested why and how our toys, books, and games were actually helping their children learn skills essential for mastering the three R's later.

When I returned to work after my maternity leave, I saw the center from a different perspective—through the eyes of a new mother. One afternoon as I was going down the line of cots waking up two-year-olds from their naps, it struck me how little time they had to make the transition from sleeping to waking, a transition even many adults make with difficulty. Three of them were crying for their mommies.

I was depressed the rest of the day. It hit me hard: We simply were not meeting the needs of the children; we were meeting the needs of the grown-ups. The sheer number of children made it necessary for us, the staff, to demand that these children follow our schedule, not their own. I also saw how the children had no real privacy. Young children need one-on-one. They need a sensitive, caring grown-up to applaud all their progress, to nurture their fantasy life. This was what I did for Tara and what I provided for her at home when I wasn't there.

I realized that I would not send Tara to my own center, and with this realization, I couldn't continue working there as I had, figuring that, hey, as day-care centers go, this one is good. I needed to be doing something that I could always feel right about promoting. I needed a mission.

I was fed up with answering to the government. Every year they sent out a haughty, gray-haired inspector in a knee-hugging navy skirt. Although she had no background in education, she was paid five times what I was to look around to see if we were worthy of keeping our funding. We always did—but so did centers where I knew that certain standards were not being met.

The auditors' refusal to let me buy toys for my daughter had galvanized me; I was angry. Ironically, I suppose they did me a favor. After the audit, I wasn't just planning to leave, I was plotting my escape.

Money was not the issue. My husband and I were were pretty much just scraping by, with Ed still struggling in a start-up business that manufactured motorized golf-club carriers. As far as I was concerned, it was enough that we had a roof over our heads and pasta or even just peanut butter on the table. Everything else was just a luxury and not nearly as important as the time we spent together as a family.

I loved being a mom, I loved working with children, and I loved helping other mothers learn more about parenting and early childhood skills. I was also eager to supply Tara with the "perfect" environment in which to grow up, which included, of course, all the wonderful educational playthings I knew so well. Put that together with my toy store trip for Kenny Gutman, and a light bulb the size of Milwaukee went off in my head. I didn't recognize it as such at the time, but a real vision was beginning to take shape for me. I decided I was going to open a toy store. I had to do it for myself, and I had to do it for all the parents who couldn't get the educational toys they deserved—the toys that would help them raise smarter, more confident kids.

6. Guidelines for Brain-Building Play

PLAY IS A CHILD'S WORK. It is how children learn about the world, how it functions, and what their part is in it.

Watch, for example, as children play house. They are trying to understand their own family structure as well as practicing their future roles as adults. Or watch a child building with a set of blocks. He is learning balance, practicing his hand-eye coordination (a prerequisite for reading and writing), figuring out spatial relationships, expanding his imagination, and even doing math.

One of my favorite preschool stories is about Michael, who was building a large block structure. Alan came over and asked Michael where his bedroom was. Michael looked at him in disgust. "This isn't a house," he said. "It's a place to fix cars."

"Oh," said Alan, "I can see that. But where am I going to sleep?" Children see the world from such a fresh perspective.

You are the best judge of which toys will stimulate and challenge but not frustrate your child. Observe her when she is playing. What is she trying to learn or discover? If she is continuously doing one sort of thing over and over—puzzles, for example—let her do it. She is trying to master a particular skill.

In fact, the name of my company, Discovery Toys, came about because of the important need to support our children's play, not to interfere with it. It's critically important that we play with them a lot, but we can frequently be the participants, not the directors.

Naturally, all children develop at different rates, and the best guidelines are simply that—guidelines. However, we all have what are called Windows of Learning Opportunity. These are the different times of life in which our brains best absorb specific information. For example, the best time to learn a second language is between birth and nine and a half years. If we learn a new language after about the age of ten, we will always have an accent, however slight. The chart on the next page shows you the best times to introduce certain subjects. The shaded areas represent the Windows of Learning Opportunity during which children are beginning to acquire important new skills. During these critical periods, the more opportunities your children have to experience and repeat key activities, the more efficiently their brains will work over the long run. Remember, these are just guidelines. It is never, ever too late to learn!

◻   ◻   ◻

Here are some additional developmental principles to keep in mind:

Infants. Our brain takes in all of its information through our five senses. It is key to an infant's future intelligence that you offer her many different kinds of stimulation. Look for rattles and toys that have different textures, colors, sounds, and activities.

Toddlers. It is most important to go beyond child proofing. Turn your home into a "yes" environment. In a "yes" environment, your child can freely reach out, touch, and explore his surroundings without being frequently told "No!" or "Don't touch that!" Studies show that repeatedly

THE WINDOWS OF LEARNING OPPORTUNITY

	PRENATAL	BIRTH	I YEAR OLD	
MOTOR DEVELOPMENT	TACTILE, FINE MOTOR, GROSS MOTOR			
EMOTIONAL CONTROL		SOCIAL/ EMOTIONAL, LIFE SKILLS		
VISION		VISUAL		
SOCIAL ATTACHMENT		SOCIAL/ EMOTIONAL, LIFE SKILLS		
VOCABULARY		AUDITORY, LANGUAGE		
SECOND LANGUAGE		AUDITORY, LANGUAGE		
MATH/LOGIC			CREATIVITY, THINKING/ LEARNING	
MUSIC				

	2 YEARS OLD	3 YEARS OLD	4 YEARS OLD	5-9 YEARS OLD
		AUDITORY, THINKING/ LEARNING, CREATIVITY		

KEY

TACTILE: Mouthing, touching, discriminating textures

GROSS MOTOR: Whole-body movement and coordination, agility, balance

FINE MOTOR: Eye-hand coordination and control, grasping, dexterity

SOCIAL/EMOTIONAL: Self-esteem, cooperation, building relationships, appreciating differences, self-expression

LIFE SKILLS: Personal care, responsibility, self-reliance, resourcefulness

CREATIVITY: Imagination, ingenuity, invention, creative thinking, dramatic, visual, and musical arts

VISUAL: Seeing, distinguishing images, remembering images

AUDITORY: Hearing, listening, distinguishing sounds, remembering sounds

LANGUAGE: Speaking, reading, writing, listening and comprehending, communicating thoughts and feelings

THINKING/LEARNING: Cause-and-effect relationships, forming and understanding concepts, problem solving, reasoning, memory

hearing "No," rather than offering appropriate discipline, serves only to lower a child's self-esteem and instill in him a sense of shame and failure. By contrast, hearing "Yes," "Sure," and "Go right ahead" helps children feel encouraged, worthy, and free to explore and learn. Toddlers like to take things apart, stack and destroy, roll, pound, drop, scribble, and do simple puzzles. They love to fill things with liquid and spill them, a great activity for the bathtub. Although their attention span is unbelievably short and the whole world is brand-new to them, this is a perfect time to start reading simple board books to them, even if they can concentrate for only two pages at a time.

Preschoolers. Preschoolers are beginning to have an imagination and love pretend games and dress-up. Often they don't know the difference between reality and fantasy. Therefore, when they tell you a "story," they are rarely lying. Be careful about the type of television and movies preschoolers are exposed to. Since everything is real to them, they can become much too frightened. Instead, there are scores of excellent children's picture books that offer all sorts of adventure, vocabulary, and imagination that will keep them stimulated and happy to be with you for long periods of time.

Activities with items to sort, classify, compare, and match will help them to read and write later on. Preschoolers love to build. Big wooden blocks should be a staple in every home.

Preschoolers also love to create. Paints, markers, crayons, clay, and other arts-and-crafts materials provide an important outlet for creative expression. Don't provide any models or insist that the child needs to follow instructions. At this age, coloring books can stifle creativity. All art, no matter what it looks like, is perfect, simply because they have created it.

By ages three to four, children are ready for simple, turn-taking, noncompetitive games such as Lotto or picture dominoes, which will help develop important pre-reading skills as well as providing social development.

Play for school-age children takes on a new role. As they develop a better understanding of real versus pretend and begin to be able to think somewhat abstractly by the age of eight, they can utilize play more for recreation and relaxation. With their expanding abilities of attention, memory, and perception, children of this age enjoy categorizing, ordering, and above all, collecting. As they develop the ability to problem-solve and make decisions, they love all sorts of board and card games. Good strategic games help develop logical thinking and problem-solving skills.

Their physical prowess is also developing, so they can benefit from sports toys and equipment that will encourage them to spend time outside. A variety of balls, bikes, skates, and jump ropes are still favorites.

Educational software can be a patient teacher and an important research and writing tool as well as a lot of fun. But computers, like everything in our lives, must be used in a balanced manner. Limiting computer time, just as you would limit television, helps ensure that your child engages in other important activities.

No matter what the age of your child, read, read, and read some more to them. Research shows that fifteen to twenty minutes a day is all it takes to develop a child who wants to learn to read.

Here are some ways to create a home environment that will encourage positive play:

- ❑ Provide low, open shelves where a variety of toys, objects, and books are always accessible to your child. Rotating books and toys keeps them fresh and interesting. Keep breakable, valuable, and otherwise untouchable objects on top shelves or in locked cabinets.

- ❑ Avoid toy boxes. The toys in a toy box become jumbled and broken, causing children to become frustrated and likely to lose respect for caring for their important playthings.

- ❑ Hang your child's special drawings or favorite photos at his eye level, and change them frequently.

- ❑ Bring home new objects as often as you can, but only one or two at a time. While the brain at all ages responds to novelty, children are more likely to investigate new challenges if they are surrounded by the familiar.

When you talk back and forth with your child, even an infant, you're actually helping her "train" her brain to act as the control center for thinking, learning, and planning. Here are some ways to build your child's brain through language:

❑ Get in the habit of linking language to sensory input. Although she can only babble, infancy is a good time to help her start this linking, but focus on one sense at a time: "Do your orange yams taste sweet as honey? Are those bananas rich and creamy?"

❑ Continue linking language with sensory input throughout her childhood by incorporating this type of language into your daily routines: "It's a little chilly outside. Let's put on your soft, thick blue sweater. Look at this tall, beautiful elm tree. Isn't the bark rough and scratchy against your hand? Aren't those clouds white and puffy against the bright blue of the sky?"

❑ Provide toys that get her to think while she's playing. Toys with sound or visual input improve cognitive skills, but it's important that she be able to interact with them too. Banging two pots together or making your own noises while playing with a truck is better "brain food" than pushing buttons to create electronic noises, because her own actions provide the opportunity to link cause and effect.

❑ Finally, turn everyday events into brain-building adventures. While playing at the beach, examine and talk about the huge variety of colors and shapes in the shells you discover. In the supermarket, have your child touch the milk cartons to feel how cold they are or observe the cheese display and talk about the various colors, sizes, and shapes. Buy several different cheeses so your child can experience the different tastes as well.

7. Discovery Toys Is Born

M Y VISION OF A TOY STORE was not of just another junk mart like the ones that had let me down when I was out hunting for Kenny's present. That was the problem I wanted to fix. Instead, I pictured a cozy, welcoming, wood-paneled haven for the entire family, with space for children to play with the toys that were for sale—where they could do, you might say, on-site, hands-on research. I pictured a staff not of just salespeople but of trained consultants who genuinely cared about kids.

We would hold weekly seminars and workshops about parenting. We would give detailed hourly presentations on the educational aspects of the toys. Our goal would be not simply to sell but to help parents get the most of out of toys and playtime. This project seemed to me a perfect outgrowth of my background in education and my interest in parenting. We would call the store "The Learning Place."

Soon I was talking to a commercial real-estate broker about some retail space available in an upscale shopping center near Concord called "The Willows." The Willows boasted expensive clothing stores and chic restaurants. The space had recently been home to a sporting-goods emporium and was every bit as lavish as the one in my vision.

Fortunately, I had learned somewhat earlier in life that when you have a lot of energy—which I do—and an awful lot of ideas—which I do—and even more optimism, you had better be able to do a little reality testing as well. For example, I once had a groundbreaking idea for on-site, corporate day care—which more recently has come to fruition at some companies. But the numbers for that venture didn't even begin to crunch, at least not without a totally horrendous care-giver-to-child ratio. And I once envisioned myself as a community con-sultant, working to eliminate redundancies among various community agencies in California. (Sigh.)

After two ideas that didn't work out, I could have given up. And friends and family sometimes seem to encourage you to give up rather than to try again. This discouragement often appears in the form of well-meaning advice. More than once I've heard people say, "If it were such a good idea, someone would have thought of it already." That's cer-tainly not the attitude with which I want my daughter to grow up. Think about what underlies that statement: the assumption is that everything worth doing has been done and that there's nothing new or exciting left for you or me to discover. *Don't let others' negativity keep you from your goal.*

Fortunately, because of the positive parenting I had received as a child, I had some immunity to this kind of negativity. I knew that I needed feedback. Just because people discourage you doesn't mean that you don't have a good idea. I talked to friends and co-workers about my dream of a toy store, and what I heard was "You'll be so bored you'll go out of your mind" and "What are you going to do if the store is success-ful? Start a chain?"

People were also quick to point out that start-up costs and over-head would be enormous. A commercial lease represents a serious financial commitment, and when I added payroll, utilities, and phones, it was hard to see where the money would come from to keep me afloat until I was established.

Although some of this feedback could be called knee-jerk nega-tivity, there was too much practical truth in it to ignore. And because he knew my strengths and weaknesses so well, my father was particularly persuasive. *Choose carefully whom you listen to.* One night he and my mother and my husband and I were discussing my idea over dinner. My dad, who had many years of experience in marketing, pointed out some of the difficulties with my plan to hold parenting seminars in the store. How would I advertise? Could I charge enough to make a profit? "Still," he said, "it's such a great idea—bringing educational toys to the public and teaching parents about them at the same time. What you need is a distribution channel."

I appreciated his confidence and only wished I knew what a distribution channel was.

It was then that my husband, Ed, asked, "What about the way they sell Tupperware?"

That seven-word sentence changed my life. *Sometimes ideas come framed as questions.* Ed had the business acumen, the interest, and the objectivity to give him this flash of insight.

Most people know the Tupperware drill. The Tupperware sales rep has a party in her own or someone else's home. Women gather to nosh and chat and view Tupperware products, those well-made plastic storage containers famous for keeping food fresh.

I'd finally figured out that "distribution channel" means simply a way to get products out of my hands and into those of my customers, and the Tupperware distribution model made great sense for the toys I had in mind. As my family and I discussed Ed's idea, it took more definite shape. I would recruit women to be "Educational Consultants," doing what I had once envisioned would be done by salespeople in my store. The ECs, as we started calling them then, would receive special training. They would then go into people's homes and fully demonstrate how to make the most of the developmental/educational toys we would be selling. They would function not only as salespeople but also as advisors to parents about which of our products would be best for their children. The direct-sales model—although it would add some unforeseen complications in the future—would help eliminate part of the big start-up costs. Those costs would most likely have put us out of business in the first place, had we even managed to get into business at all.

I remember this time as one of tremendous excitement. The details were coming together, and my mission/vision—to help parents raise the smartest, most self-confident kids they could—was coalescing. A short time later, that mission got me to the trade show. And that mission would get me through many a crisis, from lawsuits to near-bankruptcy to a home life that nearly fell apart.

Our concept of Educational Consultants brought a whole new aspect to this mission as well. All along I had wanted to find a way that I could have meaningful work outside the home while not compromising my daughter's well-being in any way. Now I had a way not only to do that for myself but to enable other women to do the same. As Educational Consultants with Discovery Toys, and therefore as independent businesswomen, they would not have to punch a clock according to the hours that some store or restaurant was open or that some boss insisted upon. They could always be home when their children were sick, go to the Halloween parade, volunteer for special projects in the classroom, and go on field trips. By setting their own hours, they could make phone calls and schedule demonstrations when their children were in school or when their husbands were home. If the kids were old enough, they could even join their moms for demos or other business activities.

I was discovering another way—for myself and for thousands of women.

8. Future Vision

CREATING A VISION FOR YOURSELF, which in business is some-times known as a mission statement, is the first step in moving yourself toward living your life the way you really want to. Without a vision, you simply float along, vaguely or not so vaguely unfulfilled.

A vision statement is a picture of the ideal. It can describe the perfect marriage or the perfect vacation. For our purposes, let's assume that we are talking about your vision of your "perfect" work life. Here's how to get your life unstuck and live the life you want:

Find a time and place that is just for you to dream. Sound like a lux-ury? It is—one that few of us allow ourselves. But believe it or not, you absolutely need to take time to dream about your vision, to nur-ture it, to get to know it—just as you would take time to get to know a new friend.

Setting aside that time is harder than it sounds, unless you already know how hard it is. How about a long bath every night while your husband puts the kids to bed? How about a walk? Try just turning the television off for fifteen minutes every day before you are too tired to think, and make that your dream time.

Too many of us stopped dreaming in childhood. Who knows where your dreaming will lead today? Allow yourself true, unfettered, blue-sky thinking, and you may end up places you never imagined existed.

Eliminate boundaries. Don't let considerations of time, money, or even your children's needs enter into this phase. There will be plenty of time to worry about all that later. But if you stop yourself right out of the gate with "But buying the equipment I need will take more money than I have," you foreclose too many possibilities. (It's amazing how often money turns up for a truly great idea.)

Put it in writing. If you write down your thoughts, not only will they become clearer, they will lead you to new ones. Put a notepad by your bed; carry a hand-held tape recorder with you. Don't miss any of your own ideas!

Share it with others. Some people—I'm one of them—process verbal information better than written. For this and for other reasons, you may find it helpful to find a dispassionate friend with whom to share your thoughts—someone who cares about you but has no stake in your success. Your husband, for example, may not be very objective about your goals. When you say, "I see myself teaching Spanish to adults," he may not be able to resist interjecting, "But honey, wouldn't you have to do that at night? Who's going to put Caitlin to bed?" We'll deal with this issue in chapter 32, "Enlisting Your Family's Support."

Form a vision group. In a "vision group," you and four or five other like-minded people meet to discuss one another's goals. If the members in such a group really support one another, everyone leaves feeling ready to tackle the world.

The first and foremost rule of such a group is to make no judgments. You should be able to throw anything out there, and I mean anything, with absolute confidence that no one will wrinkle his or her nose and say, "That sounds silly!" The group should understand that you are all exploring possibilities; being silly is part of that. Doesn't the proclamation, "I'm going to be a best-selling suspense writer" sound a little silly? That's what Mary Higgins Clark set out to do when she was a widowed mother of five.

The group could meet weekly or every other week and focus on one individual per week or give everyone a chance to share at each meeting. The second rule, however, is that each presenter adhere to a time limit so that everyone gets her fair share of attention. Under no circumstances let your vision group turn into therapy or into an "ain't it awful" session. It's a surprisingly easy trap to fall into.

❐   ❏   ❐

Perhaps your vision is to make sure that every church in your county has fresh flowers every Sunday morning. It all started because you are aware that your church would love to have fresh flowers every Sunday but can't afford them, and you wish you could be of service. More than likely, your church is by no means the only one with this desire. Suddenly you have a mission. You realize that you love flowers and are skilled at using them for decoration. Leaving yourself unfettered, your thoughts might go something like, "Maybe I will open a flower shop that caters only to churches. Maybe it should be nonprofit. (If you do form a nonprofit company, you can still pay yourself a reasonable salary.) Maybe my company can help ensure its mission by becoming the premier company to decorate churches with flowers for weddings that are held there. This way we will make enough money either to donate or to charge a minimal amount for fresh flowers on Sundays."

The pathways to fulfill your vision are endless. But if you start worrying about where you would get flowers before you completely fill out your vision, you won't get past the first sentence. If the vision is complete and you really want to pursue it, things like finding flowers become details—details that your clarity of vision will ensure you are able to overcome.

Your vision statement is just a beginning. But what an important beginning it is! It is the ideal toward which you strive. My vision is of a world in which kids grow up smarter because they have the right toys to play with and the right books to read and in which kids become more self-confident because their moms are inspiring role models. Allowing moms to earn as much money as they wish, to be stimulated and recognized, and to continually grow in self-confidence—while keeping their families first—is the mission that brought Discovery Toys into being and remains its guiding principle.

9. Market Research? What's That?

ALTHOUGH MY DAD, ED, AND I all loved the idea of selling toys like Tupperware, we decided we should test the concept. In November 1976, once again I borrowed a number of toys from the day-care center where I was still—but would not be for long—employed. (What can I say? It was all for a good cause.) I asked several friends to host toy parties for me. They made food and invited their friends; I lugged over the toys and demonstrated them.

The response surprised even optimistic me. The women at the parties could hardly order the toys fast enough. My plan was to fill their orders from the day-care center catalogs. As institutional suppliers, though, these manufacturers usually didn't ship for two months. That was fine for a school or a library, but not so fine for moms shopping for Christmas. Sadly, in the end, I had to return a lot of the money I'd collected.

Although I didn't understand it at the time, we were actually doing informal, and somewhat flawed, market research. First, it turned out that I was an excellent salesperson, because I believed passionately in my product and really wanted to help others. Of course, I had never sold anything in my life, so I had no idea that my enthusiasm mattered.

More importantly, November is one of the best months of the year for selling toys. The moms who hosted and came to my demos were much more likely to be receptive than they might have been in April, near tax time.

All I knew at those parties in November was that my toys and my presentation were greeted with heart-warming enthusiasm. Ed was right. Toy parties were going to be perfect for my educational and yet entertaining toys and games.

Taking kids toy shopping can be challenging, to say the least. You pack up little Mark and Caroline, take them out in the rain, and then end up having to say no more often than you say yes, because they're little kids and want everything they see. But you generally end up saying yes to quite a few more things than you intended to. As natural-born salespeople, kids are superior to any adult! You take the toys home, and once the excitement has passed, they end up in pieces in the toy box. In a large chain toy store, you sure as heck can't take the toys out and spread them around and see if they're really worthwhile.

The whole point of our parties was that moms could touch the toys, play with them, or take them apart and put them back together, if that's what they wanted to do. As a bonus, I was there to explain to the parents—dads were always welcome too, and we've seen more and more of them in recent years—the way to maximize learning and fun out of each toy.

Our demos provided yet another service—these first toy parties became informal support groups for moms, too. We all chatted and compared notes and traded ideas about our kids—and you can never do too much of that.

I learned two things from this period. The first was to trust my instincts. Although I had always been a risktaker, this was the biggest leap I had taken. My passion drove me. I felt strongly that I had identified an unmet consumer need.

The second was that as passionately as I believed in what I wanted to do, I didn't forge blindly ahead. I asked others for help; I took my time in formulating my plans; I tested the market, although in my own unscientific way.

 Find the balance between passion and planning—and then plunge in! *If you wait for a risk-free situation to come your way, you'll wait forever. But you do need to take the necessary time to assess your strengths and to consider all your options and their ramifications.* It's like having a baby. If we all waited for the "right" time, the human race would die out.

What do you want to do? Have more time for yourself and your family? Go back to school for your bachelor's or an advanced degree? Change jobs? Here is a resounding "Go for it!" You can do it! The only thing standing in your way is you, and I know you can change that. You are a talented and gifted person. We all are. You can create a great part-time job for yourself. You can find time to study. Maybe you'll take only one course a term. So what? There's no time limit!

Dream. Stretch. And see what's out there just waiting for you to find or to invent. Network among your friends, co-workers, or appropriate organizations for advice. We're all more closely linked to each other than we often realize. If you're looking for a house but you don't have a friend who's a real-estate agent, then without doubt one of your friends knows a real-estate agent or knows someone who knows someone who is; it will be the same with any help you are looking for.

Talk to people about their experiences. Seek out people who are wise but positive. Don't let knee-jerk negativity cut you off before you start. The world is full of people who will say, "But you'll be forty-nine by the time you get your first house!" You'll be forty-nine anyway. The only question is, Do you want to have a house then? *Your wildest dreams have a better chance of becoming reality if you approach them with a measure of knowledge and plenty of passion.*

At the beginning of my journey, there were many mistakes ahead—mistakes, completely unforeseen obstacles, and some simple bad luck. But all of those experiences, sooner or later, became Learning Moments.

There was also the very large matter of my family, whom I always considered more important than the business. In addition, there were some special people who helped me, and sometimes I almost felt I was the beneficiary of miracles. The adventure was about to unfold.

10. The Cutting Edge of Parenting

I T WAS SIX FLOORS UP to my family's two-bedroom apartment at
190th Street and Eighth Avenue in New York City from the late
1940s through the early 1950s. My younger sister, Beth, and I shared
one of the bedrooms. Across the street was an asphalt playground. We
lived there until I was thirteen, and I remember it as paradise.

Our Manhattan apartment didn't have Pella windows or a Weber
grill or a Mercedes in the garage. There was no garage. We didn't have a
pool or a nearby country club or even a mall. What we did have was a
neighborhood.

I could walk to the corner store for a treat or to buy something for
dinner. I walked to school and came home for lunch every day. No one
had to pack Beth and me into the car and drive for an hour to get us to a
play date; I had plenty of friends on the same block where I lived. The
many young mothers made a great support group for one another, and
they were willing to look after the neighbor's kids if somebody had to
be away from their apartment for the day. I got to know several of these
families well.

I had a sense of independence, which for me meant that I developed self-reliance and confidence. I had a sense of community and of

my ability to function in it. When you combine this with parents who are themselves self-confident and independent thinkers, you're going to grow up knowing that the world is a place you do things, not a place you hide from. *Give your child enough independence so that she grows up self-reliant and confident.*

Adding to the splendor was all that New York City had to offer. My parents took my sister and me to every cultural event they could, from Leonard Bernstein's concerts for children to Broadway plays. We went ice skating in Rockefeller Center, visited the Bronx Zoo, and climbed rocks in Central Park. We spent summers in a bungalow colony in the mountains or at the beach. (In those days, every family who could scrape together the money left the city in the summer, fleeing the annual outbreaks of polio.)

Another advantage of my upbringing was being surrounded by diversity. People were all colors, races, and religions. It didn't matter if you didn't look like a Barbie doll. It would be disingenuous to say that this was an urban utopia. But in fact there was a healthy level of acceptance of differences that helped lead to acceptance of myself.

❐   ❑   ❐

My father's name is Paul Perlowin. He graduated from Yale with a major in English and the equivalent of a minor in music composition. One of my favorite memories is of him conducting Beethoven's Eighth Symphony in the living room as the New York Philharmonic played it on our hi-fi. You might say this was his equivalent of the air guitar, but it was magical to see him so carried away by the music.

Loving music as he did, my father organized a family orchestra with my father and me on clarinet, Beth on violin, and my mother on piano. As I recall, when we played, a few neighborhood windows got closed and a few radios got turned up a little louder, but inside our apartment, the Perlowins were having a blast.

Hilda Perlowin is the remarkable woman I am proud to call my mother. She went to college at a time few women did—unless to get their MRS degree, as the joke went—and went to work before marrying my father at the age of twenty-three shortly after the end of World War II. Within a year I was born, and then, two years and one day later, my sister, Beth.

My mother stayed home to raise us. That went without saying. At least, none of us questioned it. That's what moms did, unless the family was truly struggling.

My mother is an enormously intelligent, energetic woman. You would never guess today that she is in her late seventies—or that my father is now over eighty! They look, act, and think younger than many people in their fifties. When we were young, mom was very engaged with us—playing games, helping us with craft projects—and she was active outside the home as a volunteer for several charities and as president of the PTA.

She also encouraged us in whatever we wanted to do. In an average week, I might express the desire to grow up to be a detective, a doctor, an actress, a writer, a diplomat, and an archaeologist. My mother never said, "Don't be silly—you can't do that," or even worse, "Girls don't do that." My father was equally nonsexist in his attitudes. More than once he said to me, "If you want to be president of the United States, the only thing standing in your way is you."

Stop listening to the negative messages you may have internalized.

At the same time, looking back, I recall a subtle restlessness in my mother. She would lose her temper from time to time and yell at us, and I think it was because a woman of her gifts wasn't fully challenged by staying home full time.

When I was thirteen, we left the city for the suburbs of New Jersey. Now that we were older, my mother took the opportunity to go back to school at Newark State, where she earned an advanced degree in education. She taught fifth grade for a number of years, which she loved. Then, at age fifty, she once again went back to school, this time to get a master's in psychology. She became a marriage and family counselor, and she's had a successful practice for twenty years. As a role model who continues to take risks and challenges throughout life, I could hardly have asked for anyone better.

I should not give you the impression that everything about my childhood was perfect. Ninth grade was actually unbearably painful, as junior high years are for many young people. (In those days, junior high was seventh through ninth grades.) The high schools in New York City had seriously deteriorated by the '60s, and we moved to the suburbs. Conformity always comes at a higher premium in the suburbs, and at no time does a child feel more pressure to conform than in those early teen years.

While I was new to the area, the rest of the kids had been together for eight years. While my hair was curly, everyone else's seemed fashionably long and straight. While clothes didn't hold any interest for me, everyone else went off to the mall to buy the latest styles. I became the most picked on child in the entire class. I was the last on any team and the only one never asked to dance even once during the nightmarish weeks we had dance as P.E. It didn't help a bit that my younger sister, starting in seventh grade, immediately became part of the in crowd.

My high school was much larger than the junior high, so I went to my first day of tenth grade actually looking forward to a certain degree of anonymity. I reported to my new home room, bravely toting my new book bag, my curly hair somewhat straightened after the best efforts of a local beauty shop.

I sat down and could hardly believe my good fortune when Rob, the football star of my former junior high, sat down next to me. You see, I told myself, things *are* going to be different!

Then Rob looked over and apparently realized for the first time whom he was sitting next to. "Oh, God, it's you!" he said in a voice loud enough for the entire school district to hear. "I can't sit *here!*" And he got up and moved. Although I later faced bankruptcy, nearly died in a car accident, and came to the brink of divorce, you will not doubt that this was the worst day of my life.

My father got me through it. I came home that afternoon in complete hysterics, finally beyond coping. He held me and let me cry it out. His presence, his calm, and his love helped restore my self-esteem.

 Both of my parents have been there for me when it mattered, and I share a special closeness with them to this day. *Children remember good parenting throughout their lives.*

⌐   ❏   ⌐

As I look back on my early family life, I see that I was exposed to many things that made Discovery Toys possible. My father was a marketing executive for F.R. Photographic Chemicals, Charles Besseler, and Olympus Camera. At home he often talked about work, which made us feel included in his life, and I saw how he consistently pushed for higher and better performance from himself and others.

I absorbed from him not only a strong work ethic but invaluable lessons about sales. He motivated his salespeople and provided incentives for them to do better. I also specifically remember him saying that he often saw salespeople doing too much talking. Nothing puts someone off more, he explained to me, than an overly aggressive salesperson. The key to sales is listening. Listen to what someone wants. When you know what they want, you're not "selling" to them, you're providing a needed service. Little did I know how useful that lesson would be.

Meanwhile, I saw my mother take the road seldom traveled by women of her generation. If she was aware of a glass ceiling, she did not convey that awareness to me or my sister. Among the many lessons I learned from her was that women are not limited: they can earn money, love their jobs, take responsibility for people outside the home, and still be good moms. And because she was a teacher while I attended high school, she was generally home about the same time we were. *You are the best example to your children of how parenting can someday be a good experience for them, too.*

Depending on where they live, children today can rarely go places on their own. Even if safety weren't an issue, distances would be: getting to school, seeing friends, and participating in most activities require travel by car. This makes kids dependent on adults until they're at least sixteen and often older.

But why not stay at home anyway when there's a satellite dish in the backyard and a video game in the den? Modern technology has blessed us with many more ways to connect and to educate ourselves, if we use these devices properly. But hours spent with a headphone or in an on-line chat room or sitting mesmerized by video games or television are hardly promoting the social, physical, and cognitive development of our young people.

Children are not *tabulae rasae*, blank slates, waiting for us to fill them with data. They come into the world with their own abilities and limitations, their own temperaments. I always knew I was smart, but I didn't know that I also had a learning disability, a form of dyslexia which remained undiagnosed until I was in my late thirties. This was a serious problem in school for me. There were certain subjects like math that I felt unable to comprehend. My dad spent many patient hours tutoring me. Each night I would go to bed certain that I had learned the day's lesson, and I would wake up the next morning a complete blank. My teachers sometimes called me lazy or an underachiever, but my parents always told me that as long as I was doing my best, I was admirable. That—and my father's and mother's ongoing messages that I was a smart, capable person—helped me compensate to a great extent for this difficulty. This is the difference that strong parenting can make. ***The kind of parent you are will have enormous impact on who your child becomes.***

Parents today need to fill the gap left by the disappearance of the neighborhood and the resultant loss of the sense of community that many of us grew up with. We also need to show children that we care enough to know how they spend their time.

Most of all, we need to spend time being truly engaged with our kids and let them see that we value this time more than anything else. Since so many women have gone back to work full time, I realize this is easier said than done—which is exactly why I feel so strongly about more of us creating our own lucrative and fulfilling part-time jobs. Becoming a Discovery Toys Educational Consultant is one path, but there are literally limitless numbers of ways to create a career that is perfect for you and your family. You already have the talent and the ability. All you need is to have enough faith in yourself to take the plunge.

❐   ❑   ❐

When I launched Discovery Toys, I created a vehicle for women to pass along some of the most important lessons of my childhood to their own children. Our ECs' kids see their moms setting goals and stretching to achieve them. Kids learn by their parents' examples that self-motivation and self-reliance can be tapped to produce desired results—whether those results are in selling toys, contributing to the family budget, making new friends, or developing new interests.

I've seen families transformed. Mom is a little isolated, a little stifled, and not as happy as she would like to be. She becomes an EC. Suddenly she's got places to go, people to meet, a product she believes in, and lots of validation from the outside world. Her good feelings affect the entire family.

ECs are essentially in business for themselves, so their children get all the benefits of the entrepreneurial model: Mom taking charge, responsibility, and chances. At the same time, because she's in business for herself, she can make her own hours and set her own income goals. She can always put her family first.

In your life you must take charge, take responsibility, and take chances.

I did not put all these goals into words for myself at the time. But I know it is a legacy of how I grew up, and I would like to thank my parents from the deepest part of me.

11. Paths Taken

AT THE AGE OF SEVENTEEN, I was a counselor-in-training at one of the New Jersey Y camps located, oddly enough, in upstate New York. One of my responsibilities was to serve meals in the dining room. It was a miserable job because I hated the hot, smelly kitchen and the heavy trays. I managed to knock over water pitchers and forgot to serve entire courses. Finally, the camp administration, whose mission is to help teens grow, not to fire them, took pity on me and assigned me to wait on the staff table. They must have thought that the grown-ups would cut me a little more slack than the kids.

On my first day at the new tables, I was bringing the great bowls of camp food—pasta and peas—on a tray which was so heavy that once again I was afraid I would drop everything.

And then I almost did. I was looking at a young man my own age. Although he was seated, I could see that he was tall and sturdily built. He had a healthy tan and a shock of sandy hair. He saw me struggle to lower the tray onto the table, and he asked, "Are you all right?" speaking in a rich baritone flavored with an East European accent.

I had just met the love of my life, Ed Nemeth.

Ed had been at the Y camp for the past several summers. He was too old to be a camper but wasn't interested in becoming a counselor-in-training. Ed, however, was a genius with tools and nearly every type of repair, so it was natural for him to move into a maintenance position, and he was spending the summer keeping the whole camp glued together.

On the day of our first meeting, I was mostly concerned with hiding my emotions—and not spilling spaghetti in his lap. My attempt at concealing my interest worked a little too well. In the days immediately following this encounter, Ed gave no indication that he remembered who I was.

But I am not someone who is easily discouraged. I learned that Ed loved fresh fruit. On my first day off, I ran into town and bought as much fruit as I could afford.

That night was movie night, and Ed ran the projector. I immediately sat down next to him. He gave me a lukewarm reception at best. But when I told him that I had big stores of fresh fruit in my tent, I finally got his attention. Gradually we became boyfriend and girlfriend, although that certainly was not part of his original plan.

In the fall, I started college at the University of Pittsburgh. There is an endless debate about who wrote whom first, but Ed and I kept in touch throughout our college years, writing letters, talking on the phone, and seeing each other during vacations and summers. From the first day I had seen him at the counselors' table, I knew that I wanted to spend my life with him. I don't think that Ed was as sure of that so early on. But by the time I graduated from college in the spring of 1968, I had convinced him that we were destined for each other—another example, I hope, of how persistence can pay off.

Ed and I were married in June of that year. The ceremony was at my parents' home in South Orange, New Jersey. I wore a knee-length white dress; eighty friends and family attended and enjoyed a lavish buffet.

After the reception, we left for our honeymoon—to a rather untraditional spot: Nova Scotia, an interesting Canadian province, although not a place I would recommend for a honeymoon. Nevertheless, we had a wonderful time. Although I enjoyed my wedding and honeymoon—I guess you can call me retro—I do dream of someday putting on an enormous traditional bash for my own daughter, complete with a fancy, floor-length white gown with a long train and a veil to the floor, two live bands, and an elegant sit-down dinner. My husband will no doubt encourage her to elope.

Ed's parents, his sister (who was one of my bridesmaids), and his maternal grandmother were the only members of his family at our ceremony; almost all of his relatives had been murdered in the concentration camps during World War II. Ed's parents escaped because they were living in what was Palestine at the time. Ed was born there after the war, and his parents returned to Hungary for a visit to show off their new baby boy. Unfortunately, they were immediately trapped behind the Iron Curtain. Because they were both highly educated, the choice they were given was simple: go to work for the government—or go to jail.

During the revolution of 1956, Ed and his family were smuggled out of the country while hidden in big mail sacks on a train bound for Austria. I can only imagine how his parents felt that night, praying that Ed's four-year-old sister wouldn't make too much noise. Or what it was like for them to walk across minefields on the Hungarian/Austrian border at night. Or, later, to live in a refugee camp in the dead of winter without enough warm clothes, food, or even the ten cents required to use the bathroom.

Ed makes me think of Nietzsche's famous remark, "What doesn't destroy me, makes me stronger." He arrived in America at the age of twelve, learned English, and later earned a master's degree in physics. But it would be hard to imagine that such experiences wouldn't have some lingering effect on a boy. Essentially, Ed had his childhood ripped from him, and he often felt like an outsider with an extra burden to prove himself.

Ed and I are only two months apart in age, but I had skipped a year of junior high—no love lost there!—so while I had my undergraduate degree, Ed had another year to go. A dutiful newlywed, I took the highest-paying job available and went to work for New York City Social Services, in their Bedford-Stuyvesant branch, at the time the poorest and most dangerous area in New York City. Although it paid well, I'm afraid I didn't like it very much—actually, I hated it beyond description—but as soon as Ed graduated, he looked for a job and found one with Edison. We moved to New Jersey, and I went to work for New Jersey Bell Telephone as part of a group that hired all their nonmanagement personnel.

Although I acquired some excellent interviewing techniques, the business world didn't thrill me either. I decided the academic world was more fun, and I went back to Seton Hall to earn my master's in education.

Looking back, one can see the many times a particular path chosen affects an entire destiny. I had also applied to and been accepted at Columbia University for a degree in college administration. Although I loved the idea of attending such a prestigious graduate school and could see myself as a college president someday, I just didn't want to commute to New York every day. Apparently I was destined for something else.

While I was in graduate school, I picked up an interesting part-time job. I knew a young woman who was running a Jazzercise program at a local YWCA, and she was looking for someone to baby-sit the kids of the women who attended her classes.

What started out as a part-time baby-sitting gig soon turned into an early learning center for the kids. My boss gave me a lot of freedom, and as the number of children for whom I was responsible grew, I organized a variety of programs for the kids. I even found a woman who was willing to let us use her swimming pool for a small fee, and I taught swimming there in the summer.

I was studying education, after all, and the program became my private lab. But I think this was also when I first detected my entrepreneurial spirit. To me, an entrepreneur isn't someone who makes a lot of money or even a lot of widgets. An entrepreneur is just how I describe our ECs: It's someone who takes charge, responsibility, and chances, and who makes something happen. *Entrepreneurism is an approach to life.*

I loved the freedom I had to try new ideas, the creativity I could express by inventing new projects and building up something of my own. The program was small, but it was mine, and I loved it. But by far the biggest thrill for me was that I felt we were making a difference in the lives of the children we touched.

12. Go West, Young Woman

At home, ed and i were feeling a little crowded. Now that we lived in New Jersey, we were geographically close to both sets of parents. That was fine, as we both dearly loved our parents—but it left us feeling a little hovered over. At the slightest sneeze, Ed's mom would appear lugging gallons of chicken soup. My dad had turned his workshop into a furniture factory on our behalf. Occasionally there was some tension over which set of parents we would visit on a Sunday.

Ed and I were young, newly married, and eager to prove our independence. So when Ed was accepted to the master's program in physics at the University of Oregon in Eugene, it was an easy decision to go. It didn't matter to us Easterners that Eugene seemed like a town out of *Little House on the Prairie*. And indeed we felt like pioneers as we drove west for ten days with all our belongings packed into our dilapidated secondhand Rambler and a small U-Haul.

Ed got settled in school pretty quickly, but it was a tougher transition for me. September 1972 was the height of a teacher glut. With so many Oregon teachers unemployed, someone from out of state like me stood more or less zippo chance of getting a job, in spite of my hard-won master's degree.

I ended up working in a day-care center for $1.50 an hour, a pretty pathetic sum even in the early '70s. We lived in married-student housing—functional quarters with metal doors, the greatest luxury of which was our very own toilet and rust-stained shower stall.

Even with relatively low rent, we just couldn't make it on what we earned. For a while, we had to go on food stamps. I can still picture the rust-colored ink of those coupons. I am glad that this help is available for the people who need it, when they need it. But I didn't want to need it. Our weekly trip to the supermarket, something I used to enjoy, had turned into a trip of humiliation. I spent more than a few weekends looking through the classifieds, moaning to Ed about the teacher glut and feeling sorry for myself.

These are the times that challenge us all. It's easy to blame the economy, bad luck, or cruel bosses for our setbacks, and we've all fallen into that trap occasionally. But you have to extricate yourself, and after a while, that's exactly what I did.

I went to see the head of the Social Services Department in Lane County, Oregon. After all, I thought, I had worked in social services in the Big Apple. A small city like Eugene must be just waiting for me to arrive. Looking back, I am absolutely amazed at my arrogance—or was it simply self-confidence? Either way, I think the director must have been so surprised that I would even ask to see him that he let me make an appointment before he had time to wonder why he should. He recommended that I take the state civil-service exam, which was the only way I could be hired. I did. Six months later, I ended up working for the state welfare department, checking on welfare patients in nursing homes.

I finally was earning more than $1.50 an hour, but nursing homes at their best aren't uplifting places, and the nursing homes I was visiting were far from the best. After three months, I was literally having nightmares, both about the job and about quitting the job.

Then one day the administrator got everyone in the entire department—hundreds of us—together. He told us that the state was starting a new unit because mental hospitals were closing down and mentally ill adults were going to be placed in foster homes—an entirely new concept. He needed someone to head up this unit, someone who would be willing to speak in public in order to recruit these foster families for adults. I almost felt as though I were out of my body as I watched my hand go up.

Some say that fear of public speaking surpasses the fear of death. For me, at least right after I got this job, that statement was frighteningly true. I figured I might survive if I put together a slide show with a script I could follow as well as an exhaustive brochure that would fully explain the program. This way I could stand in the dark where no one could see me and I wouldn't even have to answer any questions. Unfortunately, I discovered that there was absolutely no budget for what I perceived to be an innovative idea. Undaunted, and because nothing could possibly be worse than actually speaking in front of an audience, I decided to approach the film and industrial-arts departments at the university—some lucky student was going to have a stimulating audio-visual project.

In the end, because of my fear, I got my brochures and audiovisual material done for free, and they were superb! I also learned an enormous amount in the process of putting them together with the students. Nevertheless, eventually I had to face my fear. I couldn't get away with just slides and brochures forever. Nice try, though! Over time, I've come to love public speaking. In fact, public speaking has become one of the most valuable skills I have today. ***The skills you acquire today my pay off in unexpected ways in the future.***

It was not a swift transformation. In all my time working for the state welfare department, I never got up in front of a group without my hands shaking and a voice in my head asking, "How the heck did you

ever get yourself in this situation, Lane?" But I would get up there anyway, and now that I speak about something I believe in so passionately, I love every minute of it, although I still get the jitters.

❐   ❑   ❐

This brings me to a crucial part of the learning process of which young
people aren't always aware. In the early years of my working life, I had
a variety of jobs. I gained different abilities from each one. At times I
felt I was drifting, but if you do your work conscientiously, there will
always be areas in which to hone your skills. I had learned interviewing at the phone company and entrepreneurship at the Y. Finally—at
the state welfare department, ironically—I tackled public speaking.
And in Oregon I had another chance to learn the most valuable lesson

 of all: ***There are opportunities around every corner—but you
must look carefully to find them.*** It's a way of living and of looking at things that keeps me afloat to this day.

 ***If you wonder what your skills or talents are, just review
your work and your life. You will discover that you have
acquired far more than you think.***

❐   ❑   ❐

When Ed graduated, our time in Oregon drew to a close. I was sad. I had
come to love my last job, and we had made many friends. But new and
significantly less rainy skies beckoned.

13. California, Here We Come

ED RECEIVED HIS MASTER'S in physics, but jobs in his field were impossible to find in Eugene. It turned out that my parents were moving to the San Francisco Bay area at the same time. My father had done business with Japan for most of his professional life. He had been the first person to import single-lens reflex cameras from Japan. He even learned to speak Japanese! Now he was teaming up with a Japanese company to manufacture and import a new kind of mechanized golf cart. No longer would golfers have to lug their heavy bags across the links—my dad's cart had a motor and was self-propelling.

Ed, being a genius at all things mechanical, seemed a natural to help run the business, which they called Pacifica. So we all reunited in sunny California. My parents bought a house in Diablo, high on a hill, complete with a stable, where they lodged two horses. Ed and I, still young and struggling, rented a tiny house in nearby Concord with a concrete backyard, consoling ourselves that since there was no lawn, we wouldn't have to spend time maintaining it.

In spite of my upbringing, societal messages were so strong that I still believed in the traditional marriage: the man takes the professional lead and the woman follows, helping in any way she can by making her own money and/or raising the children—but always deferring to his needs and choices. Although Ed never took me for granted or treated me as if I were an appendage in his life, that was the model that surrounded me. And somewhere in the back of my mind, this model was beginning to trouble me.

For the time being, though, I was happy to be near my parents again, relieved to get a break from the heavy rains of Oregon, and ready to start looking around for a new job. I knew that Pacifica was a risky venture, as manufacturing ventures usually are, and that we would be well-advised to have another income source.

There was no equivalent in California to what I had been doing in Oregon, so that was out of the question. In the end, I found myself back in day care, this time as the head teacher at a day-care center in Pittsburgh, a small town in Contra Costa county.

Things did not go well for me in Pittsburgh. I clashed with the administration on key philosophical issues involving how to care for the children. Seeking some validation for my beliefs, I decided to take some child-development classes at our local community college. On registration day, I stopped in the bathroom—and broke down crying. In front of the sink, my head in my hands, I felt a pair of strong, friendly arms encircle me. I looked up. The arms belonged to an ample and beautiful woman who was about ten years older than I. It was Sue Nurock.

"What's troubling you, honey?" she asked gently.

I felt pretty silly, of course, crying in the bathroom like a sixth-grader. But right there I gave this woman, who had been a stranger only fifteen seconds before, a brief history of my life, culminating in my troubles at the day-care center.

"Honey," Sue said, "I think you know you can trust your heart."

I really believe that God sent Sue to me that day. Not only was she a teacher at the college, but she was in charge of the day-care center there that functioned as a lab for students who were earning associate degrees in child development! She became a valuable professional contact for me, and a dear, close friend. But that was the least of it. I had reached a crisis point, and I honestly think that if I hadn't seen Sue in the bathroom that day, I would have left childcare as a profession forever.

Instead, I changed jobs. I left the Pittsburgh center behind and found a much better job as the director of the Concord Child Care Center.

No one does it all alone; we all need help sometimes. You only look silly when you don't ask for it.

❏　❏　❏

"I'll change all the diapers. We can buy baby clothes secondhand."

It happens in many marriages that one partner is ready to have a child before the other is, and that was the case for me and Ed. Sue Nurock's encouragement to trust my heart not only galvanized my work but made me realize that I really wanted to have a baby of my own. Ed wanted one, too—just not at that precise moment. Pacifica was dangerously underfunded. While the basic idea for the golf cart was sound, it still had technical glitches.

Somewhere during my patchwork of jobs, I had picked up some good debating skills. I was finally able to make Ed realize that there would be no convenient time to have a baby. At any point in our lives there would be a big disruption, so why wait? He agreed, reluctantly.

Tara was born in October 1975, a happy, healthy baby who was going to get my full attention from that moment on.

As I've already related, I didn't stop to consider whether or not to go back to work; rather, I just assumed that I was going to be a full-time mom. This was what my own mother had done, and it was, quite simply, what I wanted to do, too. Material goods were not an issue for me; I was too much in love with my new daughter to care about anything else.

All I was really concerned about was putting food on the table and paying rent, and Ed's income, fortunately, took care of that.

For many women, however, money is a big part of this decision—a decision that has many ramifications for themselves and their loved ones. So I feel it's worth taking some time to consider here.

Most experts will tell you that marriages pivot over the issues of money and sex. We can save sex for another book and acknowledge how money—who earns it and how, who spends it and on what—can cause such painful controversy. That's particularly true after a couple become parents, and even more so when two incomes are reduced to one when one of the partners decides to stay home. While almost everyone will agree that staying home to raise a child is very demanding work—anyone who doesn't agree needs only to spend a day doing it—mothers are not traditionally paid a salary.

If you are a double-income family, the arrival of the first baby is going to cause some disruption to the family finances. If mom stays home to care for the child, her income is lost; if she chooses to go back to work, then an outsider is caring for her baby, also reducing her income significantly.

Here's where the emotions enter in. Dad may feel pressure at the prospect of being the family's sole support, and why not? In all the fracas about the injustices done to women, not enough has been said about the responsibilities placed on men, who it is assumed can and should support a family, usually without help.

If mom and dad decide that mom needs to keep working, she may resent it—though perhaps unconsciously—and long for the ability to stay home and be with her children as her own mother may have done. She might spend agonizing hours feeling guilty about working full time.

These emotions can also play out in reverse. If dad thinks his child needs mom at home, she may resent giving up her financial independence and the power that such independence usually gives a woman in a relationship, or it might be that she simply loves her career.

If one partner does choose to stay at home, it doesn't necessarily have to be the woman. Freed from having to fulfill stereotypical roles, many more dads would probably opt to be the full-time caregiver.

In the next chapter, let's put all the emotions aside and talk about cold, hard figures.

14. Working May Cost More Than You Think

NEW PARENTS DON'T ALWAYS REALIZE that whether or not mom works often doesn't have as big an impact on the family budget as they think it will. A working mother's income is taxable, and childcare; except for an insignificant credit, is not deductible. For example, if a woman is earning $40,000 a year, federal and state taxes, Social Security, health-benefit contributions, etc., usually reduce that to $25,000 or less, while childcare can easily be as high as $10,000 (this figure will vary widely; it's far more if you want a one-on-one caregiver), leaving approximately $15,000. From this less-than-impressive profit, one must further subtract the additional costs associated with a job, such as commuting, eating out, and maintaining a professional wardrobe.

Everyone's situation is different. Health benefits, employee discounts, and other perks have to be factored into the plus column. The point—and it is a crucial point—is that money earned is usually significantly less than it looks on the surface, especially once the costs of childcare become part of the picture. Unless you realize this, money can become a smoke screen for other family issues. Mom may say, "Poor me, I need to work," when she might really mean, "I know this will be hard on all of us, and I do feel guilty, but I really want to go back to work." Or Dad may say, "Poor me, I have to support the whole family," when he really means, "If you're staying home all day relaxing"—he said it, I didn't—"why can't I have some time alone when I first come home or more home-cooked meals." It works much better when everyone opens up and together takes an honest look at what everyone really wants and needs.

Sharpen a pencil and closely examine the family budget to see just what that second income means. Is it the mortgage—or is it the difference between a tropical vacation and one at the local lake? Is it the grocery bill—or is it the difference between shopping at Nordstrom or Clothes for Less?

When you understand how much money you actually get to keep and where it's going, you are equipped to make a fully informed decision—one in which you can be truthful with yourself.

If you think that you can't afford to quit your job and stay home with your kids (or start a home-based business), you may be surprised. Fill in the worksheet below to see what you're really making. Not all these costs will apply to your current job, and there may be others you'll want to include.

CAN YOU AFFORD TO WORK?

START WITH YOUR TAKE-HOME PAY: $_____
That's the money you bring home after all deductions,
not just federal and state taxes.

ADD THE EQUIVALENT OF YOUR BENEFITS:

Medical insurance (+) $_____
If your job is providing medical insurance for your family,
add what the cost would be to purchase medical insurance.

Retirement or profit-sharing accounts (+) $_____
Company contributions

SUBTOTAL: $_____

Childcare (-) $_____

Business wardrobe (-) $_____

Be sure to include dry-cleaning costs, and don't forget nylons!

Lunches out (-) $_____

Commuting costs (-) $_____

*Include bus or train fare, or gas and depreciation
on car, tolls, and parking.*

Take-out food (-) $_____

*Include the pizza you order or the prepared
deli food you pick up on the way home because
you don't have the time or energy to make dinner.*

Unreimbursed travel expenses (-) $_____

*There are almost always out-of-pocket expenses above what
your company will reimburse or the per diem they pay.*

Requests for contributions (-) $_____

*How often does someone come around the office asking you to buy
raffle tickets, candy, or wrapping paper to support a charity or
soccer team? How often do you kick in for birthday or shower gifts?*

Cost of paying retail for everything, including groceries (-) $_____

You never have time to shop the sales!

Household chores (-) $_____

*Are you paying a professional to do your yard work or other household
chores when you could hire a much less expensive high school kid to
do them, if you were home to supervise, or do them yourself?*

SUBTOTAL (EXPENSES): $_____

TOTAL (ACTUAL PAY): $_____

DIVIDE BY THE NUMBER OF HOURS IT TAKES TO WORK,
COMMUTE, AND DROP OFF AND PICK UP YOUR KIDS: _____ HOURS

FINAL HOURLY WAGE: $_____

After you have subtracted all of these items from your take-home pay and divided your actual pay by the real number of hours it takes to have a job, that is, your commute time plus the extra time it takes to drop off and pick up your kids from day care, suddenly a nine-to-five job may be more like eight-to-six or even seven-to-seven, and you will be shocked to discover how little you're really making. Compare that to what you could earn in a home-based business—and then consider some of the pluses of a home-based business: flexibility, independence, and the ability to decide what income you want to make. The risk may well seem worth it.

⊓   ❑   ⊓

During the first six months of her life, Tara and I were constantly together. We bonded in a way that exceeded my hopes, which is saying a lot when you remember that I had a great deal of hands-on experience with babies.

After the first five months, when my total exhaustion began to lessen, things suddenly began to feel different. I had been to school for many years, held down a lot of jobs, and opened many doors. Now, at home with soap operas and game shows on the tube, I felt somewhat restless and unchallenged. I had to admit to myself that I was too ambitious a woman to stay home with a baby full time. But I wasn't about to work full time either. I was on the horns of the proverbial dilemma.

I know many women who discover they love the daily rituals of early childhood, and frankly, I envy them. I wish I could have been one of them. There's healing beauty in the routine: breakfast, walk to the store, play at the park, visit friends, stroll home for lunch, read stories before nap. (I'm sure it didn't help that Tara never took a nap unless she was in my arms.)

"Trust your heart," Sue Nurock had told me, and it was excellent advice. Putting the financial issue in its proper perspective makes that easier. Still, motherhood and work must be one of the most difficult juggling acts of the late twentieth century.

I went back to work only part time for a year and then started my own company, once again working part time until my daughter was in first grade. I was discovering my own way. What I didn't realize was that I was going to discover a new way for a lot of women, a way that they too could, amazingly, keep those many balls in the air.

15. Childcare Options

FOR THE WORKING MOM—whether she has a home-based business or is working full or part time outside the house—good childcare is the linchpin of daily life.

You need to feel confident that your children are being well cared for, and your children need to feel comfortable with their childcare provider. There are essentially five kinds of childcare; which one you choose depends on your hours, your finances, and your child's age and temperament.

Relatives. Extended family is a gift to everyone. Lucky indeed is the mother who has a mother (or father, or sister, or aunt) who will help with the children. A relative who is a caregiver is someone you know and trust. They might even work for free!

Sadly, the grandparent-as-caregiver is a vanishing phenomenon in modern America, due in part to the way families move around and in part to the feminist movement: the modern grandma might be working herself or just enjoying her life. She might feel that since she has already brought her own children up, she has no further obligation.

As a mother, you must be cautious, too. Just because this pro-posed caregiver is related to you doesn't mean that she has the same values which you do—or the same patience or energy. The mother who raised you so well is a bit older now, and running after a toddler is darn hard work. And if you *didn't* like the way she raised you, realize that she is unlikely to do things differently with a grandchild.

Ask yourself, is this relative someone who you would hire if she weren't a relative? If not, don't leave your child with her for long periods, even if this leads to some hurt feelings.

Au pair or nanny. An au pair is a young woman from another country, generally in her early twenties, who wants to see the United States but can't afford to do so without help. So she takes a job for six months to a year, and at the end of her commitment spends time traveling around the country.

Theoretically, a nanny is someone who has gone to school to learn to be a caregiver. She has more training and more commitment to the job as a career; she will also be more expensive.

Many women go to work as full-time childcare providers without any formal training. Years of school aren't necessary, but prior experi-ence is extremely helpful. And you should look for someone certified in CPR. Don't fret about this; you could offer to send your nanny to a local CPR class and to a basic infant-safety class. (Call the Red Cross for information.)

Au pairs usually live in, and often nannies do as well. Room and board are part of the salary—a bonus for you, if you have the space. Some couples worry about losing their privacy—but it seems to me that your privacy is a thing of the past as soon as your first child is born!

The biggest advantage to having an au pair or a nanny is that your child receives one-on-one attention, something especially crucial in the early years.

Another is flexibility. Should you and your husband be out late, the nanny will be sleeping at your home anyway, so you won't need a baby-sitter. Should you happen to be a bit late getting home from work, well, she's already at home.

To keep everyone happy, however, you have to be careful not to take advantage of this situation. Some states have laws in protecting nannies and au pairs from being exploited by their employers. Occasionally I've seen a parent who thought that she had acquired an in-house slave. Wherever she's from and however old she is, an au pair's time is something you need to respect. After all, she's taking care of the most precious person or people in your life. There are many more jobs available than there are good helpers. Should you mistreat your nanny, she can easily find a better situation. Meanwhile, a change in caregivers is very difficult for a child.

The pitfalls work both ways. I have also heard complaints of young, untrained women who come to this country mostly looking to party instead of responsibly taking care of the babies in their charge. One way to avoid trouble is to make expectations about hours and duties clear to everyone, put them in writing, and have all parties involved sign the document. So, for example, if you expect occasional night work, include that in the contract. This way, if problems do arise, you have something concrete to refer to.

This setup can work fabulously, as it did for us. Only three women lived with us while Tara was growing up. Each one stayed for many years, and they all are still an important part of our family.

Share care and baby-sitting co-ops. With share care, two families hire one caregiver to take care of two or possibly more children. Each family pays a little less than they would to hire someone by themselves, but the caregiver still earns a little more than she would if she were taking care of one. The caregiver may watch the children in her own home or come to one of her employers' or rotate between the two families she works for.

If everyone is compatible, not only do you save money, but your child gets a companion. The disadvantages may be obvious: you have less control over the situation and your child won't always come first or be in his own environment. Of greatest concern, however, is that when children are very young, the caregiver may find it difficult to manage them together.

Baby-sitting co-ops are formed by a group of mothers who take turns watching all of each other's children. This situation usually works best for short periods, such as when two families agree to switch off baby-sitting responsibilities on Saturday nights so that all the kids stay at one house while the other parents go out for the evening, and the reverse the following week. It would be the rare and very dedicated woman who could manage this for regular work hours over the long haul. However, that's just what some women did during World War II when many moms were working and day care was hard to find.

In-home day care. These are intimate settings, often with no more than six children and sometimes as few as three. The day-care provider may be a woman with her own child who wishes to stay home and earn money; if she has the right temperament for it, everyone benefits.

The homelike setting is pleasant, and the frequent mix in ages among the children can be a plus, since younger ones love to be with and imitate older children. If there's a backyard, and if the provider has help, the children will have a chance to make good use of the outdoors.

In-home day care is less expensive than one-on-one care. But there are things to watch out for. An in-home provider is less likely to have the resources to purchase large quantities of craft supplies and educational toys or to have a really good outdoor play structure. Whether or not the mom has enough patience and training to handle so many children at one time by herself is certainly something you'll need to investigate.

Make sure the in-home center you send your child to is licensed. Licensing covers some important areas such as fire exits, maximum number of children allowed, and some other safety issues. (Day-care providers are not allowed to put children in mechanical swings, for example.) A licensed day-care provider is also likely to have had not just CPR and basic safety training but at least a seminar or two in early childhood development. But licensing does not address how your child's time is spent or the philosophy of the owners. It's fine with the state if your kid spends six hours of his day watching television.

This is where you come in. Plan to drop by at least once a month, at different times during the day. (This applies to any childcare situation you decide upon.) I have included a comprehensive list of questions at the end of this chapter that will help you evaluate the ideology and practices of in-home day care as well as larger centers. There's also a list of some signs to look for in your child that may indicate if there's a problem with the quality of care the provider is giving.

Day-care centers. Day-care centers are much larger than in-home day care—there's anywhere from twelve to several hundred children. They may be run by corporations or be nonprofit. In the latter case, they usually are subsidized by a church, charity, or the government.

There are many positives to day-care centers. They are likely to have more resources than in-homes for equipment and supplies; they provide a gregarious child plenty of opportunities to socialize and develop important verbal skills; the director and teachers usually have some training and credentials. In short, if a day-care center in your community has been around for a while and has a decent reputation, you can send your child there with reasonable confidence that he'll be well cared for.

There are some downsides, however, to even the very best day care. First of all, a child's time there is generally highly structured. Because of the large number of children for whom each teacher is responsible, there isn't a lot of downtime for kids who might need some. Generally there's no privacy and little, if any, real individualized attention. The creative child who likes some time just to dream, or the quiet child who enjoys individual play, rarely has the opportunity to simply relax and do what he wants.

As part of that structure, children need to eat, sleep, and play when they're told. Most kids find some routine reassuring; some kids actually thrive on it. But almost all will find there are days when they're not sleepy at nap time, when they're not hungry at lunch time, or when they just don't feel like painting at craft time. At some point during the day they may need to be outdoors to work off their physical restlessness—but outdoor play is generally confined to a prescribed schedule that may not match theirs.

Most disturbingly, the ratio of children to teachers is such that, especially in the case of infants, it's almost inevitable that there is a baby in distress. In Massachusetts, for example, as in most states, the law allows a ratio of three infants to one adult, or seven to two adults. No two adults, no matter how caring, can minister effectively to seven babies at once.

Another serious issue is the turnover in staff. Day-care workers are among the lowest paid in the country, sometimes at or below the poverty line; it takes superhuman dedication to stay at such a job. Meanwhile, your child may be learning that she can't allow herself to get too attached to people who might be gone next week.

❐   ❏   ❐

Here is a comprehensive list of questions to ask a prospective in-home childcare provider, a share-care giver, the director of a day-care center, or a caregiver who will come to your home. Included are philosophical questions aimed at finding out how your childcare provider really works with children, as well as specific questions you need to ask a day-care center.

First, here are a few tips: When possible, ask open-ended, probing questions. You'll get much more information and will find out what your prospective candidate really thinks and feels. Close-ended questions tend to telegraph what you want to hear and can often be answered with a yes or no. An open-ended question is, "What would you do if my child grabbed a toy from another child?" A close-ended question is, "I believe in spanking my child's hands"—which, by the way, I don't—"when she grabs a toy from another child, don't you?"

People are nervous when being interviewed, even if they don't show it. Find a comfortable, informal setting for the interview. Allow yourself five to ten minutes for chitchat so the candidate can settle down. And of course, always offer something to drink. Nerves often make people thirsty.

It is common for the interviewer to talk too much during an interview. This is a hard habit to break, as we are all socialized to share our thoughts and feelings with one another. Let your candidate do all the talking, even if you totally agree or disagree with her point of view. Asking questions and responding with encouraging remarks only—"I see what you mean" or "Tell me more about that"—is the only way to gain a real sense of who you are about to hire. If you telegraph your beliefs by becoming too enthusiastic or too unhappy, a smart person will figure out, consciously or unconsciously, how you feel and will react accordingly. It is far better to find out your candidates' real philosophies during your interview than after he or she has made your child unhappy.

Allow at least one hour for your interview. You can always cut it short, but you may not have the time to extend it. You will probably want to interview your first choice a second time. Things always look different, either better or worse, the second time around.

On a more prosaic note, write your questions down before you do the interview. Don't trust yourself to remember them all in what may actually be a stressful situation because you're contemplating separation from your child.

Any or all of these questions may be used. Do not tie yourself down to following your list exactly. If your candidate is talking about an interesting topic, continue down that path. If you do wander—and you probably will—the list will come in handy to get back on track.

A few of these questions obviously apply only to an in-home or home day-care situation. Most of them are useful to ask both the day-care-center teacher who will be caring for your child as well as the director. Her philosophy is extremely important even though she will not be dealing with your child on a day-to-day basis.

Finally, check references thoroughly. It is very important to find out what the references didn't like about your candidate. For most of us, it's easy to give good references, but you need to know the problems as well. If you like the candidate but hear some things that concern you, make sure to get her side as well. (Don't forget not to lead her.)

Questions of philosophy

Why did you become a teacher, au pair, etc?

What other experiences have you had with children?

Tell me about your own family.

What will your past references say that they didn't like about you?

What do you consider your greatest strength?

What can a child do that will frustrate you?

How do you react when you are frustrated?

How do you feel about children watching television or (if appropriate) playing with the computer or video games?

Do you think there should be any limits on the amount of time they spend doing these activities? If yes, how long, and how would you ensure these time limits are enforced?

Describe your favorite boss. Describe the worst boss you've ever had.

What do you want to do after you leave our family—or the childcare profession?

Questions of discipline

What kinds of behavior in children do you consider "bad"?

What kinds of discipline do you generally use when a child misbehaves? (If time-outs are one of the methods that come up, find out how long they last, where the child is placed for a time-out, and whether she or he can come out before the time is up, and if not, how they will let the child know how much time has passed.)

Let's say my child refused to leave the park when it was time to go. What would you do?

Is there anything more serious you would do if the situation warrants it? If yes, describe a situation that would warrant such an action.

How would you handle the following situations with my child: Had a temper tantrum? Hit another child? Refused to take a nap? Refused to eat his meal? Was hungry in-between meals? Doesn't want to eat the food you have prepared and wants something else? Wet his pants? Refused to wash his hands before eating? (As part of this list, be sure to describe any typical problems your child creates for you.)

Questions of the potty

Do you toilet train children at the center?

How would you go about toilet training a child?

At what age would you start?

Do you think there is any difference in age readiness between boys and girls?

Is it acceptable for my child to wear diapers to school? If so, how often do you change her? Is there a specific age at which you will no longer allow diapers?

What if a child who was already trained wet her pants?

How would you react if she told you she had to go to the bathroom in the store but really just wanted to see the bathroom?

What would you do if she refused to use the bathroom at home but announced she had to go five minutes after you left the house?

Questions of transition

Do you have any suggestions for helping my child make the transition from being with me during the day to being with you?

Do you think it is likely that he will be upset when I leave?

How long do you think this upset will last? How will you take care of his concern or upset about my leaving?

How best can we communicate with one another about my child's issues and progress?

Is it OK with you to work for me, for pay, for two to three weeks while I am still at home?

Miscellaneous but important questions

What would you do in a medical emergency?

Have you (or your staff) had training in child CPR or first aid?

How do you feel about my child using a pacifier/blanket/bottle? (The time of day is an important issue to discuss. Some people and day-care providers are comfortable letting their children use any or all of these items at any time, others at only specific times. By the way, the average age for a child to stop sucking his thumb naturally is eight. Children have a need to suck much longer than we think.)

Do you have rules about sugar (junk food) in a child's diet?

Do you have a valid driver's license? When I check with Motor Vehicles, will I find anything on your driving record?

(Other issues you need to discuss include working hours; having friends come to visit; whose car, if any, she will be using; availability for evening work, generally for extra pay; and any other household chores you expect to be done during the day.)

Additional questions to ask a day-care-center director or home day-care provider

What is your child/teacher ratio? Does this include only your teaching staff, or others, such as the director, secretary, or janitor?

What credentials and education do you and/or your staff have?

How many of your staff have been with you for more than two years? Less than one? (Turnover is quite difficult for young children.)

What do you do if a child becomes ill during the day?

What sort of outside activities do you provide?

Are the children free to wander outside at will, or are there specified times?

How do you encourage creative expression?

How do you introduce new skills to your children?

Do you have group as well as individual activities for the children? Give me some examples.

Do you introduce music, drama, and other cultures to the children? If so, how?

Do you have learning centers? What are some examples? Are they permanent or do they vary each day?

Can children choose among various learning centers, or do they all need to participate in one?

May I see a copy of the last three weeks' curriculum?

Do you supply breakfast, lunch, or snacks, or do I?

Does my child have an individual storage place to keep his things?

If she gets wet and no longer has her own change of clothes available, what will you do?

What is your criteria for advancing children from one class to another? (Are they looking for developmental signs or simply promoting by age?)

Any suggestions for helping my child make the transition to your school?

May I observe before I place my child here?

May I drop in anytime to observe my child in her classroom?

16. Transitions: Helping Your Child Adjust to Childcare

IMAGINE THAT YOU HAVE BEEN a stay-at-home mom for the past five years. One day, just as you finish putting your clothes on, a giant grabs you from behind, carries you downstairs, straps you into a restraining device, and transports you to a law firm. "There," he says, pointing to a desk, "you are a paralegal now."

You turn around and try to leave, but the giant blocks your path. "You must stay," he booms.

So you sit at the desk. You don't know anybody, you don't know what a paralegal does, you don't know where to get yourself a cup of coffee or even whether you're allowed to leave your desk to get one. You know that you're expected to behave and do your job, but what is required to do either of those things? All you can do is pray that this is a bad dream and that you're going to wake up very soon.

Now imagine instead that after five years as a stay-at-home mom you decide it's time to go back to work. You feel a little fearful about the transition, so you attend a two-day seminar at a nearby community college addressing the concerns of reentry women. Now better fortified, you put together your résumé and begin to network by calling former co-workers. To your delight you learn that your former boss wants you back so badly that he's willing to give you flextime, perhaps even Fridays off. You return to work on your terms, feeling happy and comfortable. (Probably this is still a dream, but it's a much nicer one.)

OK, which way would you like to have it?

Adults usually make the transition back to work somewhere between these two extremes. To my knowledge, there haven't been many sightings of paralegal-kidnapping giants lately. The point is that adults have control over how we handle our transitions. Children do not. They rely on us to make those transitions smooth for them.

My story of the giant and the paralegal, obviously, is a metaphor for how it can feel to your child when you go back to work and she suddenly finds her familiar daily routine completely changed. Whether she is starting day care or being cared for by a nanny, the upheaval is enormous. She is no longer at home, or she is at home with a stranger. Everything is different, and she's uncertain as to what's expected of her. How can you make her experience more like my second example?

Besides your natural desire to see your child happy, there are practical benefits to getting your child successfully settled as well. It is much easier to address any problems at the beginning than it is to make a change later when you are back at work and both of you are quite possibly overwhelmed.

Here is the process I recommend. It may seem daunting, and you may not be able to follow it to the letter. But remember that this is an investment in your child's well-being and sense of security. It will make your life much easier as well; nothing is worse than being at work every day and worrying about your child.

❑ Give yourself two to three weeks to accomplish the transition—more for a child who is having difficulty, less for others who, usually for reasons of temperament, simply adapt more easily.

❑ If you are planning to go back to work when your child is very young, i.e., less than six months old, I strongly recommend that you select a childcare situation before the baby is born. You will have enough to do—recovering from childbirth, adjusting to motherhood, coping with sleepless nights, preparing to return to your job—without that additional burden.

❑ Plan to make several visits with your child to the center (or in-home day care) together. Stay with him the entire time. The first visit might be for only half an hour, unless he wants to stay longer. Make each successive visit longer until they last several hours.

❑ Once your child is comfortable in this new setting (and you should be, too, having had ample time to observe its functioning), you can begin to leave him there for short periods. For a twelve-month-old, you might start with a fifteen-minute absence; for a two-year-old, half an hour is a good guideline; for a three-year-old, you might even try an hour. (These times are suggestions only; you will have a sense of just how long your child can tolerate at that moment, and some of it will depend on whether and how much he's been left in the care of others up to that point.)

❑ If you will have an au pair, nanny, or baby-sitter coming to your home, then do the same thing in reverse, i.e., have her come to your home for increasingly longer periods over the course of several days or weeks while you remain in the home. When your child has adjusted to this step, you can begin to leave him on his own with your caregiver for short periods.

❑ When you leave, always say good-bye to your child and explain that you will return shortly. It will be helpful if you can link your return to a specific event (when lunch starts, when recess is over, after he wakes up from his nap), since young children don't grasp the concept of minutes and hours.

❑ Never, under any condition, sneak out without saying good-bye. That will leave your child feeling abandoned and truly fearful that you will never return. Don't do that to him anywhere—not at home or even at Grandma's house.

❑ When you say you are leaving, you must go through with it, even if he fusses or cries.

❑ Repeat this process over a period of several days, each day staying away longer. (You must adapt this process to accommodate an infant, whose conscious understanding is less. Still, babies very much know the difference between familiar and unfamiliar surroundings, so frequent visits are useful; similarly, leaving for increasingly longer periods reassures them that you will always return eventually.)

❑ Gauge by your child's response how quickly you can increase your absences. But whether the process is fast or slow, if your child is in the right environment, eventually she will be happily waving good-bye to you in the morning. If after a full month or two she still doesn't seem to have adjusted and is still in hysteria when you're gone for the normal amount of time each day, and if there are no specific changes or unusual tensions at home, you need to reassess the placement. What is a perfect situation for one child can be intolerable for another. If, after an adjustment is made, your happy child appears to regress and becomes upset when you leave or refuses to go at all, then you will want to make sure that everything is all right with the current arrangements. Something may well be wrong. It might be very small and fixable or something large and untenable. Since he can't tell you, you have to be a detective and find out yourself.

❐   ❑   ❐

Occasions like the birth of a new baby—or even a stay-at-home sick sibling—can cause a child to become reluctant to go to childcare. In that case, I say, why not let him stay home with you (and his sibling) for a few weeks? There will be plenty of time for him to "have" to go to school.

If keeping him home is not feasible, then be sure to acknowledge his reluctance without judgment. "I understand that you don't want to go to day care today. You wish you could stay home with mommy, too. You think I love the baby more than you. I love you just as much as the baby, and I am looking forward to seeing you after school." Don't get into an argument. You can't win. Just reflect his feelings and continue to repeat that you are looking forward to seeing him after school. You may have to go through this scenario every day for a while. It's worth the effort to spend some extra time reflecting your child's feelings, as well as helping him identify them, while still remaining firm about your decision. Eventually he will accept leaving you, if not happily, at least not feeling unloved. Two books that may help you improve this skill are *Between Parent and Child,* by Haim Ginott, and *How to Talk So Kids Will Listen and Listen So Kids Will Talk,* by Adele Faber and Elaine Mazlish.

17. Signs That Your Child Is Not Thriving in Childcare

THE QUESTIONS IN CHAPTER 15 make for getting your child an excellent start in day care. Hopefully you will ferret out likely problems ahead of time and therefore make the "right" choice from the start. However, even after you have done all your homework, you may find your child in a situation that just isn't right for him, even if it was perfect for his sibling(s).

Sometimes our children fool us. Once they have decent language skills, they may sound like they can tell us if anything is wrong. Unfortunately, children up to the age of six, or even older, have difficulty verbalizing their feelings, especially when it is not about a specific incident. Often, they are unable to even identify their feelings. (We probably all know certain adults who struggle with identifying, let alone expressing, their emotions.) We need to monitor our children's behavior in order to discover what they are feeling.

Is your child suddenly weepy? Is he reluctant to go to childcare, when he used to be happy? Does she suddenly have bad dreams? Is he suddenly becoming more aggressive with his siblings or friends? Is he withdrawing from family or friends? Is she much quieter or noisier than normal? Is she suddenly fearful of strangers, relatives, or even a parent? Does he have significantly more tantrums than usual? Has he suddenly become combative?

These symptoms may be a result of something going on at home: the birth of a new baby, the new baby starting to crawl and becoming a threat to your older child's possessions, an illness or death in the family, a new sitter, or a new teacher at school. Any unusual tension in the home will also be reflected in your child's behavior. If there is unusual stress or tension, it is helpful to alert your childcare provider.

There is no need to overreact to any of these symptoms. Any or all of them can be caused by the developmental stage your child is in and may be completely normal. I relied heavily on these books: *Child Behavior: The Classic Childcare Manual from the Gesell Institute of Human Development*, by Frances L. Ilg and Louise B. Ames; the "Ages and Stages" section in *Touchpoints: Your Child's Emotional and Behavioral Development*, by T. Berry Brazelton, M.D.; *Your Baby and Child: From Birth to Age Five*, by Penelope Leach and Jenny Matthews; and *Caring for Your School-Age Child: Ages 5 to 12*, edited by Edward L. Schor. These were wonderful resources when there were sudden changes in my daughter. Tara, as do many children at times, used to go to sleep a perfectly "normal" child one evening and wake up the next day a child I had never met. After a while, I learned that these phases generally last about ten days to three weeks, and when they depart, a whole new skill or thinking process appears. For further information on these and other parenting books I recommend, please see the resources.

However, you don't want to "underreact" either. There may be a problem with your childcare that you need to know about. A child's symptoms exist on a continuum from mild to severe, and what is wrong, if anything, will similarly range from mild to severe. Your child's upset, if it is childcare-related, may be because he didn't get to play with the toy he wanted that day; or because the center is not equipped well enough and she's bored; or because the day-care mom allows too much television; or because he doesn't like the lunches and therefore is getting hungry later in the day; or because a serious bully on the playground is having a severe emotional impact on his self-esteem.

At the extremes, there could be a serious lack of personal attention on one end of the spectrum or entirely too much attention, including physical and/or sexual abuse, on the other end. Although much hyped in the media, incidents of abuse are fairly rare. If it happens to your child, though, it might as well have happened to the entire world. If you suspect any form of abuse, see your pediatrician immediately and get a referral for a highly qualified child psychologist.

Most toddlers and preschoolers are prone to bruises and other minor injuries. (I've even heard the expression "toddler legs.") Often this age child is more curious than coordinated, and it's actually good to see them try to climb a little higher or run a little faster than they could before, even if the result is the occasional boo-boo. If, however, these injuries seem to be occurring much more frequently than you think is appropriate, you may have reason for concern. Talk to the teacher or caregiver. It may just be the number of children around and the opportunity for more adventurous play than at home—or there may be something more serious going on. (Injuries can be inflicted not just by adults but by other children as well.)

Never ignore your instincts about your child. No one, neither relative, pediatrician, friend, nor teacher, knows your child like you do. If I had not allowed Tara's teachers to tell me I was being overprotective and overly concerned when I expressed my belief each year that she had a form of dyslexia, we would have had her tested by an educational psychologist much earlier than fifth grade. The earlier you can intervene with a child who is learning disabled, the more you can help. It's only because of my formal training, knowledge, and Discovery Toys products that I knew she wasn't having the typical scholastic difficulties most children encounter. Most, if not all, learning-disabled children also have some social problems, but that is a topic for another book. If you are concerned, it is worth the money to have your child tested by a professional. The schools generally do not have the resources to do a thorough diagnosis. Check your insurance policy. If private testing is prescribed by your pediatrician, sometimes your insurance will pay some or all of the cost.

If you think something is troubling your child, don't let anybody simply reassure you. Find out for yourself. Go home, or to the day-care home or center, frequently and unannounced at different times of the day for at least one month. Being a little overcautious is a heck of a lot better than living to regret letting something go that you shouldn't have.

In all cases, whether your child exhibits disturbing behavior or seems to be thriving, you absolutely need to drop in at least once a month, at various times of the day, unannounced, to observe the situation. That way you can feel absolutely certain that your childcare situation is the right one for your child. After all, isn't our children's well-being our most important job?

18. Hi, Grandma!

I N APRIL 1977, I was biding my time at the day-care center, mad as heck that I couldn't buy the toys I wanted and burning with desire to start the toy company that will change the world.

Right at this time my grandmother called. Grandma Liz was my father's mother: four feet and nine inches, buxom, curly-haired, and still active in her late eighties. Grandma had always been a big part of our lives. When my sister, Beth, and I were young, she would ride the subway from Brooklyn once a week to take over at home and give my mother the day off. Later, I would spend several weeks visiting my grandparents at the summer house they rented each year in Long Beach, Long Island, New York; these were some of the happiest times of my childhood.

"Hello, Lane?"

"Hi, Grandma!" I greeted her when I recognized her voice. This was funny, though. Usually Grandma waited for me to call her.

"Honey, your father tells me that you want to start a toy store."

"Not really a toy store," I said. My grandmother was a very sharp woman, but I wasn't sure how much she wanted to hear about direct sales and distribution channels. "But we're really excited about it, and—"

"Could you use a little extra money?"

In the past ten thousand years of civilization, has the answer to that question ever been "No"? I hesitated. It was such a generous, unanticipated offer. I hated to take money from my grandmother, but I wanted to start this business very, very badly. Ed and I had no savings; we didn't own our home.

"I guess I could."

"How much?"

"Five thousand dollars?"

This was not a number that I came to after doing a business plan or consulting a CPA. In fact, it was just a nice round figure that I pulled out of the air.

"I'm so delighted I can help you in this way," she said.

"I'd be thrilled to accept that from you, Grandma, but only as a loan, and I *will* pay you back, just not right away." She was not a wealthy woman, and this was a big deal for both of us. "OK, honey. I'm going to cash in one of my savings bonds."

That's exactly what she did. Two weeks later, I received a $5,000 check from Elizabeth Perlowin made out to Lane Nemeth. I deposited it with many emotions. My grandmother wasn't just giving me money, she was telling me that she believed in me. I was not only touched by her faith, I was motivated by it. My business had to succeed now because I could never let Grandma Liz down.

Allow people who love you to support you, if they offer from their hearts. Money can be more than money; it can be an expression of their faith in you, and that is a priceless gift.

Some of Grandma Liz's money went for the plane tickets to get Sue and me down to that toy trade show in Los Angeles; more of it paid for our hotel. So, thanks to Grandma and my last-minute triumph over my nerves, Sue and I were finally in the ballroom of the Biltmore Hotel. Just as at any trade show, the show floor was divided into booth and display areas that were rented by various manufacturers, distributors, and suppliers. Boxes and boxes of toys towered above us, neon pink and green and yellow, with exploding clouds and twirling skirts and big, big happy smiling faces of children.

Sue and I felt like kids again ourselves. Dazzled by the lights and color, we ran excitedly from booth to booth—only to discover that these towering displays were often nothing but boxes—I mean literally nothing but boxes; some of the manufacturers had not even bothered to bring the toys, just the boxes that the toys would come in! While there may have been practical reasons for that, to me it confirmed the message that the toy industry was about packaging, not toys.

Again, as with my ill-fated shopping trip on behalf of Kenny Gutman, I could see that the intent was that the box itself sell the toy. The boxes were what it was about. Pictured on the outside were exotic action shots and detailed photos of battleships for the boys' toys, and wistful, romantic photos of fashion dolls in perfect kitchens for the girls'. And on the inside was some little cheap plastic thing that vaguely resembled the photo and had too-small parts that never quite fit together the way they were supposed to. Age-appropriateness was not, and to this day is not, based on any child-development standards I had ever heard of. (See chapter 6, "Guidelines for Brain-Building Play.")

Depending on your age, you may remember this phenomenon from your early years as a parent or even from your own childhood. Sue knew it well, and now that I was a civilian, I was learning about it all too quickly. Mom or Dad or Grandma would buy little Tiffany or Colin the big splashy box that promised ever so many thrills. On Christmas or his birthday he would open it, often discovering that the product itself was usually only half the size of the box. Then he might discover that the toy simply did not do what had been promised on the endless advertising that bombarded him every six minutes while he tried to watch cartoons. The "hours of fun" promised by the manufacturer was frequently more like weeks and weeks of anticipation followed by a minute or two of fun.

As Sue and I continued to make our rounds, we tried opening some of the boxes to check out the contents, only to have some vendors become angry at us for messing up their displays or perhaps for thinking that the toy inside had anything to do with what they were selling!

I was dispirited, and yet the sensory input in this vast, crowded space enthralled me. This was only a regional toy show, relatively small compared to many others. But it was my first, and I thought it was awesome. This was raw commerce. Sellers were ballyhooing their wares like the money changers in the temple. Paradoxically, that aspect of it also struck me as inappropriate. I was so alive with my vision—the idea of bringing high-quality, fun, educational toys and games to kids, toys that they would not only love but learn from—that listening to these men hawking big plastic weapons of mass destruction and noodle-thin platinum-haired fashion dolls offended me. Goodness knows we all have to make a living. But there was something so pure and unsullied to me about what I wanted to do. Children have always needed toys, and in the late twentieth century, parents were not about to stay home carving elaborate acrobats that perform when the two sticks they sit between are squeezed together. Toy manufacturers were taking advantage of their captive audience; the industry was fat and complacent.

Afloat on this sea of junk, I kept thinking of the potential. I couldn't be the only mother in America who wanted to change all this, who wanted to see something fun that was also intelligently designed to promote a child's development.

It was in this complicated spirit of dismay and excitement that we stumbled onto Richard Bendett's toy booth. We saw immediately that Mr. Bendett's inventory was a little different. Smaller, more modestly illustrated boxes previewed games that looked like the kinds of things

I was using in my day-care center. Inconveniently, as with so many others, the boxes were tightly packaged in shrink-wrap. Mr. Bendett was busy with another customer. Sue looked at me and said, "We don't have time to wait. Let's just sit down and open them."

Believe it or not, that's exactly what we did. Right on the floor in the middle of his booth, we started to unwrap, open, and play with all his games.

Sue and I were ecstatic. We had finally found what we had come for: fun, exciting, educational products.

"Uh . . . ladies? Exactly what do you think you're doing?" We looked up at an unhappy, brown-haired, stocky man with glasses who was actually a very friendly person named Richard Bendett. At that moment, he sure didn't look friendly. The poor man had had his back turned for no more than a minute and two wild-haired young women had come close to dismantling his entire booth. We already had his toys and boxes everywhere, blocking access to his small, precious exhibit space and preventing people from passing through.

"We're sorry!" I was nearly delirious. "But whatever you've got— I'll take it!"

I spent almost the last of Grandma Liz's money in the next few minutes, ordering a dozen each of the fifteen items that Richard stocked. Richard recovered from hurricanes Sue and Lane, recognizing in us kindred spirits, and has been a good friend to Discovery Toys ever since. As for me, I was thrilled to discover that there were some decent toys out there, if you were willing to look. It was a good thing that I hadn't turned around at the airport.

19. So This Is for Real?

IN JUNE, TWO MONTHS after the toy show, I quit my job at the day-care center. My mother was shocked. "How are you going to pay the rent? What's going to happen to Tara?" She meant well; it was a grandmother's protectiveness. However, her own example of hard work and risktaking was a much greater influence on me than her momentary panic that I was giving up my modest but steady income. My favorite comment was from a well-intentioned friend who said, "If selling educational toys to parents is such a great idea, why isn't someone else already doing it?"

Commit fully to your vision and passion. Wear Teflon when others try to negate your dream.

I was too excited to be worried about being out on the street. But once again my enthusiasm outstripped my planning. In July, Richard Bendett's merchandise, along with about twenty-five other good toys I had unearthed by painstakingly scouring the Los Angeles show, began to arrive en masse. The UPS man and I were on a first-name basis. Ed was just as excited as I was, but climbing over boxes all the time was getting old. One day he picked up a box and it *mooed*, *baaed*, and *woofed* at him. He suggested that perhaps I needed some additional space. The boxes were everywhere. The garage, the kitchen, and even our bedroom were already full.

Later that same day, after stubbing my toe on a box of newly arrived Stack 'n' Pops, I announced, "I need some other salespeople." Clearly, I couldn't do this alone.

I began talking to everyone I met about this incredible new opportunity available to them. I couldn't believe anyone would want to pass it up. Of course, many did. Instead of being rejected, I felt sorry for the chance they had missed to change their lives. *Rejection in business is not personal. People have many reasons to say no other than you!* I also put an ad in *The Contra Costa Times* that read, "Schoolteachers Wanted to Sell Educational Toys and Games." I knew from personal experience that schoolteachers are grossly underpaid; the way we undervalue the worth our children's education made me sad then, and it makes me even sadder now. But because of that, I also knew that teachers were often looking for some supplemental income, and who better to sympathize with and understand what I wanted to accomplish? I soon started to get a few responses, and to this day Discovery Toys has a solid, highly motivated base of schoolteachers and ex-schoolteachers among many other professionals who work with us part time or have made this their career.

One of the first calls was from Bonnie Nelson. She called the house when I was out and spoke to Ed, who has a Hungarian accent. It's very sophisticated, very Charles Boyer, but in this particular instance it had an interesting effect on the listener. Here was Bonnie responding to a rather cryptic ad, and when a man with an unusual accent answered the phone, he told her that these were a new kind of toys, toys that she wouldn't have heard of before. When he invited her over to his house for a "demonstration"—at night—she became uneasy. Just what kind of "toys" were these? Was it possible that there was a white slave ring operating out of Martinez, California?

Bonnie did come to our house that night. She also brought her husband, her kids, and her golden retriever, Sam. Apparently the National Guard had refused to accompany her. She told me later what had been on her mind, and we had a good laugh, especially since Bonnie fell in love with Discovery Toys during my first demonstration and had a long, successful career with us until, sadly, she passed away in 1985.

The second of our original Three Musketeers was Kathleen Jackson, a friend of mine from Lamaze class. The third was Pat Nelson, who heard about me from a mutual friend. I was flattered by Pat's interest, especially after our mutual friend described me as "this crazy woman I know who's starting a toy business."

Nobody had an MBA. Nobody really had any business experience to speak of. So far we had business cards that said "The Learning Place" and some photocopied order forms.

But we also had an idea to which people responded immediately. Whenever I or my new Educational Consultants had a demo, moms instantly recognized that they were seeing valuable toys which they couldn't get anywhere else. So while my enthusiasm continued to race ahead, I did take some time at this point to ask around for help and advice. In fact, I think I sensed that I was on the verge of something big, and while I knew I was going to move forward at any cost, as long as it in no way hurt my daughter, I didn't want to blow it, either.

My dad was my key mentor. I was very fortunate to have a father who had spent his professional life straddling the worlds of business and creative pursuits. Always a successful marketing executive, his passion for music and the arts kept him open to new ideas, especially his daughters'. Having talked me out of the store, he now gave me the single most valuable piece of advice I'd had since Ed had evoked the name of Tupperware. He told me to collect the money with the orders.

"How can I do that," I protested, "before I deliver the goods?"

My father is patient with me at all times, so perhaps it was to emphasize his point that he responded bluntly. "Lane," he said, "you can go out of business this week or next week unless you get the cash up front. It's up to you."

In any business, after the mission, cash is king.

It was hard to argue with that pronouncement. I didn't try, even when Dad went on to explain that it had to do with cash flow. I sat there trying to look intelligent while I wondered, "What's 'cash flow'?"

Don't be afraid to seek advice from experts in areas in which you're not. Most people are happy to give advice.

We ended up asking for money with our orders. Customers never had a problem with it, and in retrospect I realize that's a significant reason why Discovery Toys is here today.

20. "Your Husband Actually Lets You Run a Business?"

BY THE FALL OF 1977, almost a year had gone by since my first jerry-rigged demos with toys "borrowed" from the day-care center. Once again, it was the best time of year to be selling toys, and although we had only a small line, we sold toys that no one else had. The four of us booked $20,000 in orders. Naturally, I was proud of myself and my Three Musketeers. I was naïve enough to believe that the hard part was over. Everyone is blind at some point in their lives!

Sometimes it's fortuitous that we don't know what lies ahead. We might be too scared to continue down a successful path if we saw the obstacles ahead of us.

In January 1978, Ed and Tara were still sharing digs with Toys-R-Lane, and while they'd both been good sports about it, I knew that if The Learning Place was here to stay and if my family was, too, it was time to take the next step: rent a warehouse.

I found a small space in Concord. It was all of nine hundred square feet, a combination warehouse and tiny office. What it lacked in size it made up for in unattractiveness. Among other problems, it had neither heat nor light. To be kind, it was a dump: home to ants and mice, and badly in need of paint. Faced with the prospect of making it my dump, though, I thought it looked like Hearst Castle.

Not so fast. The landlord didn't want to lease the space to me because I was a woman, even though my credit history was fine. I was angry, and I argued with him at some length but got nowhere. It may be hard to believe, twenty years later, that someone would be so openly prejudiced. Today most landlords would at least have the sense to come up with a different rationale rather than risk being sued. This gentleman, however, was quite clear about his feelings. No woman tenants, no way. Perhaps he was afraid that during a particularly bad bout of PMS I would paint the whole building pink. Believe me, any color paint, if it were fresh, would have been an improvement.

He finally agreed to lease me the space if Ed signed the lease, even though Ed wasn't involved in the business. At some point it did occur to me, fleetingly, to continue my difficult search. But I wanted to launch my business and did not allow myself to spend precious emotional energy on such a ridiculous individual. Ed signed the lease, and I put the incident behind me.

$ ***Don't let others' perceptions of you become your perceptions of yourself.***

I still owed my grandmother $5,000 in addition to needing to make the lease payments, so in spite of our strong fall season, I was more broke than ever. The passion was keeping us all on fire. Now that we had "corporate headquarters," we wanted a sign. This brought to a head the fact that none of us involved really loved the name "The Learning Place." It was a holdover, in part, from my original idea for a store, and most people seemed to find it stiff and dry.

I would always talk about how when children played with educational toys, they made discoveries on their own, and about how huge the difference is between being taught something and discovering it for yourself. But it was Pat Nelson who picked up on that notion and suggested that we change the name of the company to Discovery Toys. I loved the idea, and we incorporated in January 1978 as Discovery Toys, Inc.

Listen to what you're saying to others.

Thanks to Grandma Liz and a few true believers, I had gotten started, but by now I knew that I needed more money. If I'd been in business before, I would have realized it sooner, because every business needs money! In our case, we needed money to buy inventory, to print literature, and to expand.

How do most businesses get money? That's what I was asking myself in January 1978. What I learned was that they may be funded by big corporations with deep pockets, by money raised in an public stock offering, or by loans from banks or individuals. Very few businesses manage to be self-financed (which means that all their growth and operating funds come from current sales). Hewlett-Packard is an example of an extremely successful company that has remained virtually debt-free. But the vast majority have to get cash from an outside source in order to survive. Discovery Toys was comfortably in the category of the vast majority.

I went to my own bank, which seemed a logical place to start, looking for a loan. Discovery Toys was already a reality and had been doing brisk business for three whole months. But the commercial loan officer, a man just a few years older than I, hardly looked at my paperwork. He explained that we were new, that we had no track record, that we had no assets, only debt.

I was surprised. Look at our sales, I said. Look at our toys! Everyone loves them and no one else has them. We're going to be big. We're going to pay you back—I promise!

The loan officer was not about to budge. So I simply went to another bank—and another, and another, lugging armloads of documents, carefully filled out. I even brought sample toys. I was certain that one of these men would catch the fever that so many of us mothers had. But no one did. Everywhere I got the same "sorry not interested" response.

What I learned later was that it's almost impossible for any start-up company such as mine to get funding from a commercial bank. The odds are too much against small businesses. But it is in the nature of entrepreneurs to be a little egocentric, which is a not-nice way of saying that we believe in ourselves, and I was no different.

Gather information and weigh the odds. Regardless of the obstacles, stay persistent!

Although I feel much more forgiving toward these bankers with the benefit of my twenty years of experience, there was one whose response I'll never forget. This young man scanned my paperwork, glanced up to look me over, and then asked, "You mean your husband actually lets you run a business?" He added with a chuckle, "I suppose I might allow my wife to work, assuming she was home in time to cook dinner!"

21. For My Next Trick...

WHAT TO DO NEXT? The truth is, I was very lucky. My brother-in-law, Walt Weissman, expressed an interest in Discovery Toys. Walt is a brilliant businessman and an extremely generous human being, but I think his real genius lay in marrying my little sister, Beth.

My family has a nice history of marrying young and staying married. My parents have long passed the fifty-year mark, and Ed and I have celebrated our thirty-first anniversary. Beth met Walt while they were both attending the University of Wisconsin. They married while still in college, and then, when Walt was accepted to Stanford University's graduate program offering a combination M.B.A.–J.D. (law) degree, Beth was able to transfer to Stanford to finish her own undergraduate degree. She later went on to earn a Ph.D. in remedial reading and now is a well-known painter.

In 1978, Beth and Walt were living in Concord, very near me and Ed. After completing his education, Walt had immediately gone into business for himself as a market maker. A market maker buys and sells stock from his own account and makes or loses money on the spread between the bid and the asking price; Walt was already doing very well at this risky game. But to this day, Walt swears to me that he was not simply doing his sister-in-law a favor when he loaned me $50,000.

Help can come from unexpected places.

How did I come up with that amount? This time there was a method to my madness, or so I thought. I had to project inventory for the year. Having no history, I took the biggest number I could possibly imagine selling and came up with $100,000. In order to buy inventory to support this "forecast," I needed $50,000.

So now I had not only my grandmother to pay back but my brother-in-law, literally ten times over. It was, I must say, just a little bit of pressure. I deposited his check with serious heart palpitations. What if the business failed? Earning $5 an hour as a day-care-center director, it would take a lifetime to pay him back. That's if we didn't eat, pay our rent, pay our taxes, or buy clothes. At that point I decided I absolutely would not, could not fail, and whenever the thought of the possibility of failure arose again, I simply told it to be gone.

Our thoughts control our actions, not vice versa.

Walt's money kept us afloat through 1978. The end of the year brought our first real fall season, which as I had learned the hard way, would be 60 to 70 percent of our annual sales, as it is for the entire toy industry.

During 1978, we grew rapidly. My original Three Musketeers were now forty Educational Consultants. We didn't have any rewards for recruiting; nevertheless, it seemed that everyone knew someone who wanted to join us. As it has turned out, almost all our ECs have been women, though not all moms. Although we've had a few men on board over the years, I suppose most men feel that the nature of the business—home demonstrations of toys with mostly women in attendance—is a more natural fit for women. It's too bad. When our ECs hold couples parties or dads-only parties, the men are not only equally interested in the products, but they tend to spend more.

In any case, the word was spreading on its own. This was even more remarkable when you consider that these were not salaried positions. In fact, back then a new EC had to make an investment of $500 to buy the starter kit. (We have various starter kits available now for far less expense; the basic kit is under $135.) The EC would use the toys in her kit for demonstrations—she had no choice, since we had no catalogs—take orders, and then receive commissions on the orders. Working a few hours a week, an EC could make extra money; working consistent part-time hours, she could earn a substantial supplemental income.

From the start, people recognized the value of what we were doing, and that was the catalyst for our growth. The excitement was always palpable, as women came to our warehouse, picked up their kits, participated in two full days of training, and went out into the field to make their presentations. Unfortunately, they weren't always quite as excited when they came back to the warehouse to pick the same order up—twice. The first time was to get the order so they could deliver it to the hostess, and the second time was to clean up all the mistakes I had made filling the order the first time. Being dyslexic was a real interference in my ability to do that job. But I couldn't afford anyone else, so I did it all. (We didn't have a clue that we could actually use UPS.)

Interestingly enough, we've had some women buy the starter kit with the intent not to sell Discovery Toys but to simply keep the kit samples for their children, the end result being that they would have some nice toys purchased at cost. Surprisingly, many of the women who bought a kit for their own use have become involved in spite of themselves and have turned into big-selling ECs and even big-time sales directors. *You can't ever judge someone's real motivation in the beginning. Frequently they don't even know themselves.*

In that first "real" fall season, we had achieved $100,000 in orders by early October, and I still had the biggest two months of the year to go! You would think that this would be cause for pure celebration.

Unfortunately, we had ordered only $100,000 worth of toys, which were supposed to last the entire year! The orders were coming in too fast for us to even figure out what to reorder. Even had we known, toy vendors aren't able to fill many orders in November. They hope to get all of their merchandise into the stores by September.

I underwent a crash course in business administration as I learned about inventory systems—systems that we didn't have. Worst of all was our complete lack of warehouse personnel. When we could fill at least a partial order, we were six weeks late! Time was crucial, as Christmas was bearing down on us. Our forty ECs kept having parties and workshops and kept selling those toys! It was ironic that the more we sold—the more successful we were—the deeper into the mud we sank. We were simply not going to be able to fill all those orders before Christmas, which meant that customers would be disappointed and ECs would not be paid.

We live in an age of buck-passing. If our children aren't learning, it's the fault of the school system. If we get lung cancer, it's the fault of the cigarette companies for advertising too effectively. If we spill hot coffee while driving, it's the fault of the people who had the nerve to sell it to us. And if our political leaders notice some social problems, they go on television to tell us how it's all the fault of the opposition, the media, other countries—anyone but themselves.

But I was brought up to take responsibility for my actions, and I was in agony over this. Although I had not foreseen the situation, however little I might even have done to prevent it, Discovery Toys was my company, and as Harry Truman was famous for saying, the buck

stopped with me. ***You will make plenty of mistakes. You can't move ahead without them. Its OK as long as you learn from them and don't blame them on somebody else.***

By now, complaints were coming in as fast as the orders. To everyone's relief, I found a replacement for myself in the warehouse so

I could start writing personal letters of apology to every hostess who had opened her home to Discovery Toys and who was going to have to disappoint her friends. I explained that we were a new business feeling our way through our first year and that we had seriously underestimated the demand for our product. I told them that we were totally committed to addressing our problems within one year and that we were interested in their input about how to accomplish that. I even enclosed an extra toy that we did have in stock as a further token of apology.

I also contacted every one of our Educational Consultants with a similar apology. I put my heart on the line. I told them how much I appreciated all the work they had done, assured them that I truly understood how upset and angry they were, and promised that we would not repeat the debacle next year. *Two of the most powerful words in the English language, when sincerely offered, are "I'm sorry."*

All of the ECs were upset with us, to say the least. Some even figured that our grand scheme wasn't going to work out after all and left the company. Fortunately, many decided to give us another chance.

I think people responded to my honesty. In a business where your sales effort is completely out of your control, the trust between headquarters and the field isn't simply a critical part of the business, it *is* the business. Although I still regret the inventory fiasco of that '78 season, I like to think that the way we handled it laid a foundation for the solid relationship that still exists between me and the ECs today. People will figure, "If management is going to tell us the truth about their mistakes, we can believe them about anything."

22. Out of Breath or
Out of My Mind?

NOWADAYS THE WORK-VERSUS-FAMILY dilemma gets a lot of press. National magazines show photos of very pregnant women in business suits, carrying a toddler on one hip and lugging a briefcase in the other hand. A typical cover story is "Work Plus Family: Can the American Woman Have It All?"

The debate rages from the highest academic circles to the ten-second sound bite on the local news. How can a woman raise a family without giving up her career?

Feelings run hot. Feminists believe passionately that women shouldn't be shut out from job opportunities whether or not they also happen to be mothers. Conservatives insist that working mothers are damaging a whole generation of innocent children. Pragmatists try to come up with viable solutions, but the solutions themselves—job sharing, flextime, telecommuting—signify just how complex the situation is and are generally more talked about than implemented.

In 1978, I didn't have any role models to look to or any magazine articles to read. My mother's example was crucial, but even she had been a full-time mom until I was thirteen.

In the end, though, each woman and each family has to find their own way, no matter how many magazine articles get written. Here's how Ed and I worked things out:

Tara had just started preschool and was attending three mornings a week. On one of her free mornings, I would stay home with her, while Ed stayed home on the other day. On her three mornings in school, I drove her to Sunshine Preschool at 9 A.M. in nearby Pleasant Hill. Preschool started with a half-hour circle time, and Tara insisted that I stay through that entire period. After group time was over, she happily waved me away. This whittled my morning work hours down from two and a half to two. Of course, I was the only mom whose daughter insisted she stay; sometimes I even thought that by the end of the second year of group time, Sunshine should have given me a diploma, too! But I was grateful that I had the flexibility to stay with Tara when she wanted me to help her make the transition.

At 9:30 A.M., I made a dash to the office, where I'd do as much work as I could in a two-hour period. The business was growing fast, we were grossly understaffed, and it seemed that every day brought a new crisis—sorry, I mean challenge. At 11:30 A.M., I would race back to Pleasant Hill to pick up Tara, and we'd go home and have lunch together. At 1 P.M., the baby-sitter would come to the house. I would hustle on back to work, where I would stay until 5 P.M.—not a minute later, no matter what happened. I didn't care if the warehouse was on fire. Leaving at 5 P.M. got me home by 5:30 P.M. so I could be there to let the baby-sitter go home.

Tara and I then spent the next three hours together. This was the part of the day that was just for us. We would play, read, take a bath, and play some more. We called it "Mommy-and-Tara time." I didn't get on the phone, we didn't turn on the television, and we didn't even clean up. It was just for fun and interaction. ***Take your parenting hours as seriously as you do your working hours.***

I looked forward to those three hours as a retreat from the madness of a business growing like Mighty Joe Young. And I know that this discrete, special part of the day meant a lot to my relationship with my daughter, too. The routine, the predictability, helped her to feel secure; she knew she would have my undivided attention during those hours.

At 8:30 P.M., Ed would take over to put Tara to bed, and I would resume work, now at home, until the work was complete or I collapsed, whichever came first. I'll let you guess which one it usually was.

It makes my heart race to remember these days. It almost sounds as though it worked. And in all seriousness, it did, more or less. A lot of the time it was even fun; I enjoyed balancing my time between work and Tara. I'd rather be pushing myself and trying to do a little too much than sitting around bored.

Boredom was never a problem. The problem, as any working parent knows, was that there wasn't a lot of slack in the rope. My life was a precision-timed instrument. There wasn't room for mistakes, for doctor or dentist appointments, for me, or even for just sitting around to take a deep breath. I was trying to give 100 percent to my child, my husband, and my business.

But as Gene Wilder points out in the Mel Brooks movie *The Producers*, there's only 100 percent of anything. Still, you think that if you just play it right, you can make the day into twenty-six hours instead of twenty-four. Maybe you can train yourself to sleep three hours a night or to take ten-minute catnaps throughout the day, as Thomas Edison is reputed to have done. But no matter what you do, there's always a load of laundry left in the basket, homework that needs checking, and someone in the family who just lost a new raincoat.

 You're only human. Don't pretend you can do more than you can do. Make a list of all your tasks. Divide them into A, B, and C lists. Proceed to throw away the B and C list. You'll discover they really don't matter.

One way we did more or less make our lives work was that we were very clear about our priorities. If the furniture got dusty, fine. If we ate macaroni and cheese three nights in a row, fine. A life that looked like it was run by Martha Stewart wasn't as important as our real life as a family, even though my house usually looked like it was run by Abbott and Costello.

Just as crucial a part of this was that I always knew that the best people possible were taking care of Tara. Working in the childcare industry, I knew whom to look for. We had two young women who alternated spending afternoons with Tara during these early years, Toni and Tucker. I deliberately chose women who were quite different from me. Both of these wonderful ladies were much more like earth mothers and thoroughly enjoyed doing things like baking cookies with Tara and mixing up batches of homemade play-dough. (See the recipe at the end of this chapter if you'd like to make some play-dough with your child.)

They were like me in that they loved Tara dearly, had lots of patience with her, and were trained in early childhood education. One day Tucker took Tara out for lunch as a special treat. For some reason—it was quite out of character—Tara decided to throw her plate of spaghetti. Tara froze the moment she did it, totally startled that she had hit Tucker with it. She had obviously not quite realized what was going to happen— it was a true Learning Moment about cause and effect and plates of spaghetti. Fortunately, Tucker started to laugh, and Tara laughed with her. Needless to say, the incident could have been handled very differently. Tara had completed that particular "science experiment" and never repeated it. There was no point in getting angry. It was clear from her reaction that the act was not malicious in any way. She had frightened herself enough; she did not need an adult to make her feel worse. If you accidentally spill water on a friend or break a glass in their home, what would you want them to say to you?

For me, knowing not only that Tara was safe and happy but that she was being nurtured and stimulated was the only way I could walk out the door each afternoon with any peace of mind. If you're a working mom, you know about this, and it's why I've included chapter 15 on choosing appropriate childcare and questions to ask potential caregivers. It's intended to help you put your concern and your love into practical application and to help you make sure you have the right childcare situation, whether a group setting or a one-on-one. If you don't feel confident that your child is in good hands while you're gone, you might as well be home.

❐   ❐   ❐

There were other stresses to contend with. Pacifica, the business my dad had started and Ed had joined, was not doing well. My father, in fact, had decided to leave the business; he and my mother returned to the East Coast.

Ed continued to run the business, which in retrospect was a mistake. The walking, motorized golf cart was a good product, and other versions of it are quite popular today. But there was only one manufacturer capable of supplying the motor, which is always a very dangerous situation, and money was entirely too scarce. Manufacturing companies virtually eat capital. Ed was valiantly trying to keep the company afloat, but without a big infusion of capital, it was doomed. Both of us were too inexperienced, however, to realize this or to think about trying to raise the amount really needed from venture capitalists.

In August 1979, we moved from our Martinez apartment to our first home, in Pittsburgh, California. Thanks to an FHA loan and a $5,000 down payment—seemingly a magic number—that my other grandmother left us when she died, the mortgage payments were manageable at first, but they were scheduled to rise sharply in future years. Adding these payments to our lives served only to increase the pressure on us. But I felt confident that I would somehow be able to meet the increases as they came. So far, with minor breakdowns about once a quarter, when I refused to get out of bed for a day, I was handling the pressure well.

Some pressure can be healthy, even a driver in your suc-cess. The trick is knowing when the pressure is healthy and ***when it has become too great or even paralyzing.***

❐   ❑   ❐

Despite the insanity of trying to run two businesses, we put everything aside on weekends. We did it to keep us all sane and centered. We made sure that at least Saturday or Sunday, and preferably both, were our family days. My own parents had done that, and once again, the model was powerful. I cherish the memory of climbing into bed with mom and dad on weekend mornings for a leisurely snuggle while we planned a day of fun for the four of us. Beth and I could count on this wide-open space, this time when we had our parents all to ourselves, and it bred the closeness we share today. (See chapter 23, "Five Ways to Enhance Your Time with Your Child.")

Ed and I honored that tradition. We turned down any invitations that came our way and made it a day for just the three of us. Living in the San Francisco Bay area, we were surrounded by beautiful places to go: nature trails, beaches, mountains, amusement parks, and museums. But those were only a plus. It didn't really matter where we went, as long as we were together. On rainy Sundays, we stayed home and played games or had a picnic on the living-room floor. ***Take one day a week to have fun with your family, no matter how busy you become.***

Freeing your weekends can be done. It takes both planning and flexibility. All parents want the best for their children. But sometimes we get confused, overwhelmed, or even scared. We think that if we don't stay in the boss's good graces, if we don't put in that overtime, we might get fired, and then where will the family be? But when you are crystal-clear about your priorities, the fear tends to go away. You don't have to let your boss keep you from your daughter's ballet recital; if he really can't spare you for an important family event, then I suggest you look for another job. It may take some effort, but it will be worth it. There are always good jobs available if you have the patience and the courage to explore your options. Maybe you will even discover that with your talents you can create your own job and set your own hours.

You may also find that your family can live on less money than you thought was necessary. Instead of making car payments, you might manage with a secondhand car that still gets you where you need to go while making you truly rich—in time spent with your kids.

In the end, does it matter to have had a successful working life if you don't have a successful relationship with your own children?

RECIPE FOR KOOL-AID PLAY-DOUGH

2½ cups flour
½ cup salt
2 packages Kool-Aid
3 tablespoons oil
2 cups boiling water

Add the wet ingredients to the dry ones and mix. The mixture will be very hot, so wait a few minutes and then mix again. Add more flour if needed—perhaps another ½ cup to 1 cup—and mix until the dough is smooth. Add just enough flour so the dough is not sticky—but don't add too much or the cooled dough will be hard. You could also add scented body oil, tissue paper, fireplace ashes, coffee grinds, grated crayons, rock salt, rose petals, cornmeal, grated lemon or orange rinds, colored fish tank gravel, colored sand, oatmeal, or food coloring for added texture and sensory play. Have fun!

23. Five Ways to Enhance Your Time with Your Child

OUR TIME WITH OUR CHILDREN is too often limited. But no matter how much time we have, we want it to be stimulating and fun—time when we feel close to them and they feel close to us. No one ever dies wishing they had spent more time at work. But how many of us will die wishing we had spent more time with our family? Here are five ways to enhance the time—great or small—that you do spend with your child:

Play, play, play. Play is a child's work. If I get just this message across, my mission is accomplished. Play is the way that children learn about the world and how to grow up in it. With the right products, they also get the underpinnings absolutely necessary to succeed in school and, later on, in life.

Playing with your child will develop his social, physical, and cognitive skills, build his self-esteem, and increase his connection with you. Children spell love *T-I-M-E.* Playing with your child is the best and easiest way to make him feel loved.

Spending time playing with your youngster will pay big dividends when he or she is a teenager. Most teenagers will not sit down on demand and bare their souls to their parents. But as long as none of their friends are around and you have built a strong, open relationship by playing with them from early on, they'll still be willing to *play* with you. Whip out a board game—the best teen-communication device ever invented—and start playing. While you're playing, before you know it, you'll start to hear what's really on your teen's mind, either directly or indirectly.

Make games out of difficult tasks. Not only can making games turn the dull daily routine into something special, but it's also a way to find lots more playtime in a busy day.

Asking a four-year-old to clean up a messy room is the grown-up equivalent of being asked to wash all the windows on the Empire State Building in one day. You need to help—in fact, you will always do about 85 percent of it until they are much older—but you can use that time to help your child learn how to clean his room while having some fun with him. Even when he's old enough to do it by himself, a non-judgmental offer of help can lead to some extra communication time instead of battles: "Let's see how many blocks we can pick up in the next ten seconds. I wonder if you can put all your yellow race cars on the shelf before I put the green ones on." Puppets can also be terrific help during cleanup as well as a fabulous imagination-building tool. The puppet can make suggestions that your child might react negatively to if they came from you.

Many children resist bath time, but they'll look forward to it if you use it as playtime. Tara and I had tea parties, raced boats, and built bubble mountains. I also placed a large, clear, unbreakable mirror on the wall by the tub so we could do funny things with her hair when it was full of shampoo.

Having trouble getting them dressed? Offer a choice: "Would you like to wear your green shirt or your red one?" not "Would you like to get dressed now?" Asking a toddler or preschooler an open-ended question can be dangerous unless you really don't care what the answer is.

Avoid the arsenic hour. You know the time I mean. You walk in the door from work; you're tired, you're grouchy, you have phone calls to return, and you have to get dinner ready to put on the table. Your children rush to you with a mixture of joy and complaints. They throw their arms around your legs before your briefcase hits the floor. You say, "Just give me a minute, will you?" and then one of them starts crying or finds another equally annoying way to get your immediate attention.

Here's my suggestion: Before you pick your child up at day care or enter your house if they are home, take a deep breath. Forget the rest of your day and leave the rest of your life at the door. When you walk in the house, immediately put down your coat and everything else and say to them, "What would you like to do with Mom?" They may want to play a game, build with blocks, or paint a picture. If you've built a close relationship with them when they're young, then, when they're older, they may simply want to sit and talk to you for a while. If not, offer to play cards or a board game, or perhaps, if you like, cook dinner together.

Give them a good solid half hour of undivided attention while doing anything they want. After that, they are likely to drift on to their own pursuits and give you the time you need to make a real dinner, hang up your coat, and make those phone calls, if you must. I always turned off the phone for the evening. That's why answering machines were invented. I often think that children's difficult behavior is tied to the ring of the phone, and most of us, somehow, are constitutionally unable not to pick up a ringing phone.

I always had a snack ready when I walked in the door—an apple, a piece of string cheese, or some crackers. By the time you get home, the kids are hungry, and that makes them cranky, too. I also got in the habit of simply leaving my coat and briefcase in the car. I wasn't going to need them until much later that night, and it was a way of reminding myself to leave my work behind. Try giving this undiluted time to your kids, and I guarantee you'll be amazed at how it changes your entire evening.

Practice active listening. Active listening means to listen without judgments and to feed back what you've heard.

Your six-year-old daughter rushes in crying and screams, "I hate my brother." Your first reaction might be, "No, you don't hate your brother!" Strong emotions elicit strong emotions. Denying her feelings only serves to invalidate her as a person. Our feelings are always acceptable. It's our actions that are not.

Instead, reflect back what you've just heard: "I can see you're very angry at your brother."

"Mom, he stole my crayons!"

"And you don't like it when he steals your crayons."

"Yeah, he has his own crayons. Why should he have mine?"

By now, brother has joined the fray: "She has more crayons than I do! And hers are a lot better!"

"I hear you. You think your sister has better crayons than you do. You really wish you had her crayons." No matter how tempting, it's useless to point out that at one point they both had exactly the same crayons but she takes better care of hers. This will only cause brother to feel that you are siding with his sister. This isn't about anyone being right or wrong; it's about helping your kids talk out, rather than act out, their feelings and learn to solve their own problems. Keep listening neutrally, let both parties continue to express their frustrations, and when things calm down, let them find a solution.

The best book I have ever read on this subject is *Siblings without Rivalry: How to Help Your Children Live Together So You Can Live Too*, by Adele Faber and Elaine Mazlish.

The beauty of this? If you establish yourself as able to listen without being the judge and jury, you become a safe confidante. Ten years later, when someone offers drugs your now-sixteen-year-old daughter, she'll be able to come to you to discuss it while resisting what might otherwise become fierce peer pressure.

Be available. You can't and don't need to spend every waking minute paying attention to your child. But letting them know that you are available when they need you is crucial to their sense of security. This doesn't mean you have to cut short a phone conversation the very second your son wants a snack, though you may have to interrupt it for a moment in order to tell him that you understand he is hungry and you will be off in one minute. Then honor your commitment. If it must be much longer than a minute, I suggest you set a kitchen timer where he can easily see it and give him something to do right next to you. If you don't, the complaints are only likely to escalate. Young children have very short attention spans. They're not trying to manipulate you by getting your attention—they *need* your attention. If you give it to them freely and frequently when they are young, they will be much more able to give you time on your own as they grow.

A great book about kids that will show you when they actually can develop the ability to manipulate or control you is *The Magic Years: Understanding and Handling the Problems of Early Childhood,* by Selma H. Fraiberg.

By the way, did I mention how important it is for you to play with your kids?

EXCUSE THIS HOUSE

Some people try to hide the fact
That children shelter there
Ours boasts of it quite openly
The signs are everywhere
For smears are on the windows
Little smudges on the doors
I should apologize, I guess,
For toys strewn on the floor
But I sat down with the children
And we played, and laughed, and read
And if the doorbell doesn't shine
Their eyes will shine instead
For when at times I'm forced to choose
The one job or the other
I want to be a housewife
But first, I'll be a mother.

AUTHOR UNKNOWN

24. The Million-Dollar Headache

OW CAN YOU HAVE REVENUES of $1 million and still be going broke? Math may not have been my best subject in school, but something didn't make sense here.

Some things did make sense, and 1979 was another year of unbelievable growth. It was our second year, and very much like a baby in her second year, Discovery Toys had grown into a toddler—sometimes out of control, getting into everything, causing its parents plenty of anxiety and fatigue, but also giving them a lot of pleasure.

By the end of 1979, we had over two hundred Educational Consultants. Women often became exposed to our products for the first time when they were invited to a toy party. Many then clamored to host a demonstration and/or were interested in the opportunity we offered. Our ECs were so full of enthusiasm that they told everyone they knew about their new business with its flexible hours and its commute to the den. And in turn, many of the women they told were excited about our vision. This was especially true if they were parents. They were thrilled at the prospect of being able to earn money and yet stay at home with their kids.

At the beginning of 1979, we discovered that other companies rewarded their representatives for recruiting others into the business. In fact, we discovered that we were actually part of an entire industry called Direct Selling.

Being completely naïve about how multilevel marketing actually worked, we decided to give our ECs the princely sum of $15 whenever they recruited a new EC. Meanwhile, one of our first three Educational Consultants, Bonnie Nelson, was busy doing research into how other direct-sales companies were structured. Bonnie suggested that in addition to letting our ECs buy products at wholesale and keep the difference when they sold at retail, we should encourage them to build their own sales teams and pay them bonuses based on the sales of their groups.

We already gave free toys to the women who hosted parties and invited friends and acquaintances, so rewards were not completely foreign to us. But encouraging team-building, known in the industry as multilevel marketing, not only gave the ECs more income but was an excellent way to support women working with us who otherwise might feel isolated. It was also the beginning of a national infrastructure and the first of many compensation plans.

At the end of 1979, we were still based primarily in Northern California, although we had begun to spread through the Pacific Northwest (Oregon and Washington) and had a presence in some surprising places such as Washington, D.C. And we had sold just under $1 million in toys—and this after just two years in business!

As I've said, I had enough enthusiasm to power the borough of Manhattan. But as I've also admitted, my background was all in education. I had no business background, and I will be the first to tell you that because of this I made some near-fatal mistakes.

$$ *Find mentors and join pertinent professional associations; more experienced people can help you avoid many errors.*

In February 1979, we had moved to a new, much larger warehouse in Benicia, then an unglamorous, semi-industrial town on the edge of Contra Costa County. These quarters were only a little less shabby than our previous ones. But there was one noticeable difference: We now had ten thousand square feet—quite an increase from nine hundred—and there was also additional warehousing we could expand into, although I couldn't imagine filling up the current space.

Just having that bigger space didn't begin to solve all my problems. Why did I think it would? Just before Christmas, a friend of mine, Mike Cox, dropped by the warehouse. I had known Mike since he had knocked on the door of my first office about a year previous and had asked if I wanted to buy some miniature wooden trains that he was importing from his native England. I didn't need the trains, but Mike, a tall, dark-haired, strikingly good-looking man with a killer British accent, had a diverse background that included carpentry and sales. That first afternoon we had hit it off immediately in that marvelous way which doesn't happen often enough but feels so good when it does, and his brief sales call turned into a two-hour visit over diet sodas. Now Mike would come by every once in a while just to say "Hi."

On this particular visit in December, Mike looked around and rather casually observed, "You know, Lane, you've got way too much inventory here for a toy company, especially after its biggest selling season is over."

Don't be ridiculous, I thought, but I kept quiet. "How can that be?" I asked. "We sold just a hair under one million dollars in toys. We have to have product available for January sales. After all, these are educational toys and games. Children learn all year, not just at the holidays!" Plus I remembered that being understocked had created such a crisis the previous year.

Encourage others to tell you what they are thinking, especially when it isn't what you want to hear.

Mike explained that in a business such as mine, having too much inventory was like taking all the money that Grandma and Walt had loaned me, wrapping it in pretty tissue paper, and putting it on a shelf where it couldn't earn interest and couldn't pay salaries or rent. "Take a look at your financial statements and you'll see where the problem is," he said.

"Financial statements," I echoed. Well, I was getting financial statements all right, because I had hired an accounting firm to do them. Somewhere I had picked up the knowledge that every business needs them. The firm sent them to me three months late, but it didn't matter because they might as well have been sending me printouts of my electrocardiogram for all I could decipher them. Perhaps this was an area in which my passion eclipsed common sense. I knew we were selling like gangbusters—how could that be bad?

What was bad, as I was learning the hard way, is that the toy business—including developmental toys like ours—is highly seasonal. One of the tricks to surviving is to have just the inventory you need—not too little, because then your customers have to wait too long and go somewhere else, but not too much, because, again, that inventory is your capital and it sure isn't working for you sitting on a shelf.

$ *Most businesses have seasonal revenues; plan accordingly.*
After Mike's visit, I sat down and paid all the bills I could, and to my horror I learned that he was right. After I went through all my cash, I still owed my vendors $100,000, right after Christmas. I was totally confused; how could I have been so successful and yet in serious debt? The cash-flow monster had reared its ugly head. Yes, I was selling like crazy, but I had stocked exactly $100,000 more inventory than I had sold. Thanks to my father, we were taking money with the orders, but my markup was low, and I had commissions to pay, not to mention rent, staff salaries, and utilities, among other expenses—so although I was making a very small profit, I was completely out of

cash. Cash flow and profit, I learned as I stared at my check register, are two completely different creatures. It was another highly condensed business seminar.

Watch your cash flow above all else; lack of cash has killed many good businesses.

Since Mike Cox seemed to know so much about what I was doing wrong, I decided to hire him to help. Thank goodness I did. Mike did everything from buying us gravity rollers for the warehouse pick line—which are basically tilted rollers designed to get boxes off the shelves more efficiently—to setting up an inventory-management system. Projecting one's inventory needs, it turns out, is one-third science, one-third art, and one-third crystal ball. Even though no system is perfect, you have to at least have one.

With Mike's help, we began to get control of the problem. But we still had a $100,000 hole to dig ourselves out of, on top of my debt to my grandmother and my brother-in-law. But while I felt deeply obligated to my family, I knew they weren't going to turn the debt over to a collection agency. My vendors could; in fact, despite my huge sales and my growing team, they could have put me out of business. All they would have had to do was get together, go to court, and force me into bankruptcy to pay them off.

I had no more resources for borrowing money; banks were clearly out of the question and I couldn't go to any more family members.

Instead, I decided to go straight to the vendors to explain the situation. Most were on the East Coast, so I decided to call. It was impractical to go in person, but a letter would not do. These were just about the toughest phone calls I had ever made in my life. I was frightened almost to the point of being ill.

It often feels easier not to face a problem directly. Although sometimes being tactfully direct feels as though it will kill you, being less than direct will cause more pain to everyone involved.

You know the saying, "Feel the fear and do it anyway." It's easy to say but much harder to do. Only the fact that my unwillingness to fail was a more powerful emotion than my fear allowed me to pick up the phone and dial with shaking hands. My experience with my ECs and hostesses had also shown me that if I were honest about my mistakes, most people would also believe my sincere intention to address the problem. I believed that the vendors, too, would want to help me, not only because they were decent people but also because if I went out of business, they would get only pennies on each dollar of debt I owed them, and obviously I'd never be able to buy from them again.

 It takes a healthy, solid belief in yourself and your mission, as well as a belief in the innate goodness of people, to overcome obstacles thrown in your way.

I explained to each vendor that although we were a fairly new business, we were growing very fast and would pay them everything we owed them just as soon as we could. I was correct about their response: every single company said they would hang in there with us, and many expressed their gratitude that we were forthcoming about the problem. Responding to my honesty with honesty of their own, some even told me that had I not come clean with them, they would indeed have turned me over to collections or tried to force me into bankruptcy in order to collect. At best, I never would have been able to do business with them again—which is not my idea of the best.

By giving me more time, the vendors eventually collected every dollar I owed them—and I got to stay in business. A potential disaster turned into the foundation for lasting, positive relationships between Discovery Toys and its suppliers.

Problems don't go away if you ignore them. Instead, like an untreated wound, they can spread infection through your life.

If I had ducked my vendors' phone calls or ignored their invoices, they would have had good reason to resent me and would have been all the more motivated to close me down, even if it hurt us all. How often does a marriage fall apart because the partners don't talk about their difficulties until it's too late? How often does an employee quit her job—or get fired—because she and the boss didn't communicate about what wasn't going right?

Any lawyer will tell you that most lawsuits are filed by angry people who are more interested in getting revenge than getting good results. By the time both sides ante up attorney's fees and take time away from work, frequently everyone loses—except for the lawyers. Somewhere along the line the parties missed their opportunity to talk and to settle their differences to everyone's benefit.

I think many people struggle with communicating directly. Certainly, in this and in other areas, I was learning from my mistakes. I also looked forward to a time when those particular learning opportunities might be fewer.

25. Hit the Road, Lane

WHAT WOULD HAVE HAPPENED to Discovery Toys without Ed? Nothing, because there would have been no Discovery Toys.

Ed and I have had to face our challenges over the years. But I have been truly blessed by him in many ways, and he has given me invaluable advice at critical junctures in the development of my business.

This doesn't mean that I always recognized the value of his advice immediately. For example, in late 1979, Ed told me that I shouldn't be buying from importers; I should be going straight to the manufacturers.

"Fine," I replied. "I'm up to my follicles in debt, and by the way, the importers I'm dealing with are only five to ten times larger than I am, but I suppose this is a good time to start worrying about this."

Sometimes the hardest people to take advice from are those closest to us.

"Yes," he said, and as usual, sigh, he was right, because we were already struggling to find well-made, thoughtful toys to build our business around. I had come up with our relatively small initial line after months of turning over every rock in the American toy industry. But the essential innovation of our idea made product hard to find. We wanted the value of educational toys with the oomph of commercial ones. The educational-toy market had been traditionally limited to institutional customers like schools and day-care centers. There were many fine toys available, but they were the same every year, and when you are selling to individual consumers and want to be the one to provide Johnny with his birthday gift for three years running, you have to keep new merchandise coming. I had found that the products which combined education and fun at a price families could afford came almost exclusively from Europe. This was why I was buying through importers in the first place. I had been to the big toy show in New York, but even there, the only things I bought were from importers, too. Obviously, going to a European toy show made sense.

New York had made my first toy show at the Biltmore look like a birthday party, but the European toy shows would be even bigger. Pat Nelson, now vice president of sales, made plans to accompany me. We would travel first to the toy show in London and then go on to Nuremberg, the site of the largest annual toy show in the world.

I was scheduled to travel in February. Then, just a couple of weeks before I planned to hit the road, you might say the road hit me.

On the way home one night, for some reason I decided to take a shortcut on a more narrow, curvy road than I usually took. Making a sharp turn, my windshield was suddenly filled with the burning headlights of an oncoming car—and a head-on collision. The force was so great that my car was pushed broadside into the mountain. The other driver, I later learned, was drunk, and his car was nowhere in sight! It turned out that he had gone down the mountain, rolling over several times.

Even worse, although at least five cars drove by and saw the wreck, no one stopped. Finally a motorcyclist stopped and waited with me, helping me enormously just by his calm and friendly presence, until the police finally arrived.

Later that night, as the shock began to wear off, I discovered that my knee was badly injured—and to this day it still gives me trouble.

I had broken two teeth; I was bruised and scraped everywhere; and I had pulled what felt like all the muscles in my back. I knew that I was lucky to be alive, which made my injuries seem relatively minor, but they were also a bit inconvenient as far as a trip to Europe was concerned. Perhaps I should have canceled, but as you probably know by now, that isn't my style. So I went, sometimes getting around on crutches but mostly confined to a wheelchair, which Pat Nelson pushed.

Although I was pretty stoic about the crutches, I was less so about leaving three-year-old Tara behind for the trip. I had left her overnight only rarely, and I had never been gone for more than three days. Pat and I planned to keep the trip lean and mean, but the quickest turnaround we could manage that would encompass two European cities and let us see enough toys to make the journey worthwhile was ten days.

I probably prepared for my absence a bit overzealously. I read Tara's favorite stories onto a tape that Ed could play at night. I made a large calendar and decorated it with pictures of the three of us so Tara could check off the days until my return—the date of which was emblazoned in large red letters. I left Ed a ream of notes, instructing him on everything from Tara's nap schedule to how to launder her favorite pink sweater. Then I tucked my crutches under my arms and headed for the airport.

It turned out that my leaving was one of the most positive things I could have done. I called home at least once a day—usually more like three times—and I could hear that Ed was not following my instructional manual to the letter. In reality, it had landed in the garbage can the minute I walked out the door. One night I got ahold of him at 9 P.M. only to learn that they had just walked in the door—half an hour after Tara's bedtime! And then poor Ed—not knowing how close I already was to calling Child Protective Services—casually mentioned that he had just bought some TV dinners at the market, apparently with every intention of letting my daughter eat them! I could only imagine what other junk food she had eaten earlier.

I was distraught—no less so because I was missing Tara dreadfully. My arms ached constantly with a strong memory of holding her. I even called the airlines to see if I could book a seat on a plane coming home immediately.

But as the days passed, I became aware of something else that was happening back home: Ed and Tara were bonding in a new way. Oh, Tara missed me, too, though probably not as much as I missed her. But for the first time, Ed was completely in charge of her care. He had been a devoted father and had always done his share of diaper changing, chauffeuring, and story reading, to name but a few of the tasks that crowd a parent's day. He even stayed home from work with her one morning a week! But I was still the mother, and the truth is that I had jealously guarded my role as primary caregiver. I hadn't meant to shut Ed out, but that was the indirect result.

In my absence, Ed got to do on his own some of the fun things with Tara that I had hogged for myself—nightly baths, playing simple board games, outings to the grocery store and the duck pond—and along with the logistics he had already mastered, he got to discover how stimulating a person his little daughter could be.

Sometimes when we think we're filling our kids' needs, we're filling our own needs.

I think it's common in families that Dad worries a little less about some of the things that Mom does—things like nap times, junk food, matching clothes, combed hair, and brushed teeth. That was certainly the case at our house. I needed to let go a little bit. The words *Lane Nemeth* and *control freak* have occasionally appeared in the same sentence. But I was able to realize that if Tara ate potato chips more often than I would have chosen or if she stayed up late, it was not as important as having some special time with just her dad. I am convinced that if traveling had not been a part of my job, Ed and Tara would not have the unbreakable connection they have today.

From then on, Ed was more fully my partner in parenting; if he hadn't been before, I accept total responsibility. And when I needed to travel after that, I left with a lighter heart, knowing that Tara had a different but equally devoted parent at home.

Letting go doesn't lead to chaos—it leads to connection.
Although Tara adored her dad, she hardly ignored my comings and goings. Kids usually react more strongly to Mom's business trips than to Dad's. Is it because dads usually travel more often or are more likely the ones leaving for work every morning, or is it just that kids usually feel more emotional about their moms at this age?

Whatever the reason, it sure can make a mom's life difficult; it certainly did mine. When I occasionally had to go away during Tara's early preschool years, she would do plenty of acting out—shouting, kicking, throwing things—when I came home. When she was a little older and understood time better, she would do the same acting out before I left. (See chapter 26, "So You Want a Cooperative Child?"

One thing that helped was my talking to her openly. Heck, if I could grovel to a toy seller, I could certainly explain things to a three-year-old! She was old enough to grasp what I was saying. When she fell into one of her frequent tantrums for several days after my return, I would sit down next to her while she was on the floor. First, I always acknowledged her feelings: "I know you are angry that Mommy left you. I realize you are afraid I left because you did something wrong." (These were my words, not hers. She was too small to identify her fear, so I had to help.) Then I would repeat over and over that I hadn't left because of her, that there was nothing she could do, including having tantrums, which would make me leave her. She could be as angry as she wished and I was staying right by her side. I left because of business, finding more new toys, and I would always come back. It was exhausting for me, but I was the one who had left, and she had a right to have a reaction.

My reward came early one morning, seven tantrum-filled days after I had returned from a trip. Three-year-old Tara bounced on my bed and announced, "I've got it, Mommy. You left because of business, not because I did anything wrong. I don't have to be angry anymore. You love me."

And that was the end of the tantrums—until the next time I had to leave. Tara was just like most kids—they need constant reassurance that you would never really leave them permanently, no matter what the circumstances.

I learned other tricks for making these transitions go more smoothly. The calendar and the prerecorded stories were always useful. Ed would help her put together a book about her life spanning the time I was gone; each page was a picture about her day. And of course I called home frequently. Although at that age most children don't volunteer much about themselves over the phone, at least Tara heard my voice and knew that I was thinking about her.

Now Tara, an adult, is the one far away, and I'm the one waiting for her call.

26. So You Want a Cooperative Child?

ERE ARE SOME WAYS that you and your child can make the most of your time together:

Don't try to control everything. There are too many things to fight over, and too often parents let their own unconscious need for dominance and control lead them to create more conflict than necessary. Your children are people, too. How would you like it if someone else got to make all the rules and decisions and told you what to do all day?

You can let a lot of things go, and the end result will be that everyone is happier and no one gets hurt. Does your child want to live in a messy room? Shut the door so you don't have to see it. Too many arguments occur over this issue. After all, his bedroom is the only place in your house that is truly his. Isn't he entitled to some place he can call his own?

Does your preschooler want to pick out her own clothing? The only real reasons to object are that you—or some stranger—might think that she looks silly and you will feel embarrassed, neither of which seem like very good reasons to me to have a big fight. By allowing her to dress herself, you are fostering her independence and self-esteem.

In areas you decide are important, stay firm. The biggest reason for letting go of anything which you can let go is that there are still so many things left. You can choose what's important to you, which most likely will involve issues that can affect your child's health, safety, and cognitive or social development. But once you choose, your child must know that these rules are nonnegotiable.

Let's say you have a rule against watching television before doing homework. Your children will test you to see how firm your limits are. If you give in once, you then give them hope that you might give in next time, too. If you blow off the no-television-before-homework rule on Monday, they will push you even harder on Tuesday to blow it off again. By Wednesday you will be pulling out your hair and yelling at them. Do them and yourself a favor and keep to it on Monday. Remain calm, no matter how frustrated they are. It's easier to remain calm if you simply listen to their objections, repeat them in your words, and then continue to hold the line: "I know you think I'm a mean mom. I know you want to watch your favorite television show. I'm not the one stopping you. As soon as you finish your homework, you are free to watch it." It may take a number of times, but soon they will stop testing the rule.

When Tara was four, we went to see *Sesame Street on Ice.* I had told her in advance that she could buy any souvenir—but only one. Money was so tight that it would be an easy rule to enforce. But her friend Jocelyn's mother allowed Jocelyn to buy two souvenirs. That was too much for Tara. Standing in line for the ladies room and in front of hundreds of people, she had one of her rare—except when I traveled— but enormous tantrums. I knew that every single person in line was doing nothing but watching us. My embarrassment was at an all-time high, but I followed my normal behavior anyway. I listened to her shouts of anger and acknowledged them: "I know you want two souvenirs because Jocelyn was allowed two. You live in a very unfair home with an unfriendly mom who won't buy you another one." (I had an almost overwhelming urge to yell back, "You ungrateful child! Isn't it enough that you are here! These tickets cost me a lot of money, and I spent it so that you would have a good time, not lie here on the floor shouting at me!" That might have made me feel better for a moment, but the situation would have only deteriorated further. I reminded myself that I was the adult, and I took a deep breath.)

Finally she shouted her ultimate threat at me: "If you won't buy me another souvenir, I will sleep here." ("Fine," I thought. "See you tomorrow.")

I said, "Well, Tara, if you insist on sleeping here, then I will have to sleep here also. I don't think we will be very comfortable on this hard floor, but I certainly am not going to abandon you, no matter how angry you feel." In an instant she stood up and dried her tears.

"You would sleep with me here, Mom?" she asked in delight.

"Of course, darling. I would never leave you no matter what you did or how you were feeling."

"OK," she said, standing up, the tears all gone. "I am all better now. Who needs those silly souvenirs anyway?" And that was the last I heard on that topic.

Important note: Abandonment is one of the most primary fears that human beings have. Tara was threatening me with abandonment, the all-time worst threat she could ever imagine. Of course, she was too young to realize that it was she who could be abandoned. Had I said, "Fine, then sleep here," I would have given her serious reason not to trust me—and perhaps not to trust any adult. Never—never ever—allow your child to believe that you would leave him, no matter how angry or difficult he is. A parent who says in an angry moment, "I will leave you here if you don't . . . " has no idea of the scars he or she can create. We all need to become aware ourselves—and if possible, help others. None of us would want to intentionally hurt our children this badly.

Let them discover the natural consequences of their actions. Suppose your child is chronically late to school. You could start the morning every day by shrieking threats—or you could let him show up late. If he misses the school bus and has no way to get to school that day because you are no longer going to take him, he will have to face his teacher or the principal with an unexcused absence—not something he's likely to do more than once or twice.

However, before you change your response, make sure you find the time to have a quiet, nonjudgmental talk with him about the consequences he will face if he doesn't change his behavior. Explain that you are no longer going to argue with him about his being late for school. Tell him that he is able to make his own decision and that you are not going to give the school any excuses for him nor are you going to drive him there.

Most likely he will test your resolve the very next morning and lie in bed too long. He'll be shocked to realize that you are serious, and he may even keep the game alive for a few days more, trying every trick that has ever worked to make you take him. Once he realizes that you are serious and has to face the natural consequences once or twice, he will be on time.

Suppose your grade-schooler has to wear her soccer uniform every Saturday morning when her team competes with another. You have asked her repeatedly to please put the dirty uniform in the hamper so you don't have to go looking for it. Inform her that the next time you find it missing from the hamper on washday, you are not going to wash it. Saturday dawns and she has no uniform. Oh, well. There's no need to get into an argument, although she will surely try. Quietly remind her that she knew the consequences and chose to ignore them. The responsibility is hers, and the decision about what to do is also hers. She can go to the game wearing dirty shorts or choose to skip this one.

No matter how important the game is to her, you can't back down. That can be very hard, but it is a critical part of helping children take responsibility for their own actions. *Logical Consequences: A New Approach to Discipline*, by Rudolf Dreikurs and Loren Grey, spells out this theory clearly. Personally, I think he goes too far, but his fundamental approach is an effective way to change the family dynamics and to help your children grow. How far you choose to follow his theories is up to you.

You can help preschoolers start to take responsibility for their actions as well. For example, if he consistently refuses to help clean up a toy such as his Legos or blocks, take a carton and label it "The Disappear Box." Tell him that if he is not interested in cleaning up this toy, it clearly can't be too important to him and so the next time this happens it will go into the Disappear Box for a week. When the toy returns, if he still does not put it away, then it can disappear for a month—and eventually, if necessary, for good. The important elements here are that you make the consequences clear ahead of time, that they are appropriate to the ability of your child's development, that they naturally fit the situation, and that you follow through. It can be difficult to let go of your need to control the situation, but letting your child experience this basic cause and effect—which life will certainly teach him later and possibly at a much bigger cost—can be an important part of helping him grow up.

Reinforce the positive. Whenever you see your child doing something positive, compliment her: "That's great that you shared your doll with your sister" or "I really appreciate you putting your dishes in the sink; that helps me a lot."

Reinforcing the positive tells them what behavior is good. It also gives them more incentive to deliver that good behavior. You wouldn't want to be criticized all the time; neither does your child.

I'm always amazed to discover that some adults believe that children are just looking for a chance to get into trouble. Personally, I believe that 99 percent of our children—and with rare exceptions, grown-ups, too—want to be good. They want to be loved and accepted. They hate it when we are angry with them. Children just don't always know what "good" is! Remember, they've recently arrived on our planet, and they actually need to learn about our culture. One of our jobs as parents is to teach them while building up their self-esteem. Unfortunately, too many of us had parents who with good intentions but not enough knowledge tore down our self-esteem. It's easy to repeat the cycle. Parenting classes can be of significant help in preventing this.

Although children want to be good, they also want and must have attention in order to survive. If they can't get that attention for being good, they'll get it by making trouble. If you hear yourself yelling at your kids a lot, maybe you're not giving them enough attention for the right things. Make it a goal to ignore at least one negative behavior a day while reinforcing three positives, and see what a change occurs!

Speak to the child's behavior, not to the child. Connect on both "good" and "bad" behavior, but don't call the child good or bad. There really is no such thing as a "good" or "bad" person. We are all good inside, but sometimes our behavior is completely unacceptable. You can reinforce the positive by saying, "You are a great helper and I enjoy cleaning up with you," not "You are a good girl."

When you don't get the behavior you want, don't tell your child that he's bad. He's not. He's just doing something you don't like. Tell him what that is. Be as specific as possible—and tell him what he can do instead. Here are some examples:

❑ "Hands are for hugging and holding. If you need to hit, go and hit the pillow."

- ❏ "Teeth are for biting food. It hurts when you bite people. If you need to bite, please bite the apple or rope." (It's best to give him a specific object that he can use every time he needs to bite.)

- ❏ "Feet are for walking on. If you need to kick, please use the ball."

- ❏ "Blocks are for building with. If you need to throw, please throw the beanbag."

- ❏ "Cats and dogs are made for gentle petting, like this." (Take your child's hand and show him.) "[Name of pet] loves it when you are gentle with him."

- ❏ "Please use your quiet, indoor voice. Loud voices are for outside."

- ❏ "Chairs are for sitting on. If you wish to climb, please use the outside equipment."

- ❏ "I can see you would like a turn. You need to use your words. Please tell your friend you would like a turn when he is finished."

- ❏ "I want to help you, but I don't understand whining. Please use your pleasant voice, and I will be happy to listen."

- ❏ "Tongues are for tasting food. Please leave yours inside your mouth."

- ❏ "I know you are very angry. I will be happy to listen when you are able to use your words and tell me why you are so angry."

Don't worry about the formalities. Since children imitate your behavior, you do not need to remind them to say "please" and "thank you" when they are preschoolers; it is a difficult concept to grasp at that age. They will start doing it automatically in grade school if you have consistently modeled this behavior with them.

Take a parenting course. A parenting class can help you develop techniques that are specific to your child and can give you the additional support of being with other parents.

I've found that moms and dads are too often reluctant to take a parenting class. They feel that it's an admission of failure, that parenting should come naturally.

That's a load of horsefeathers. You had to learn to read, write, and drive, and parenting is a lot harder than any of those things. A parent who takes a parenting class is taking his or her work seriously. Most important, it can make parenting easier and more fun.

27. Trouble in Nuremberg

ALONG MY DISCOVERY TOYS journey, my naïveté sometimes was a friend to me, while at other times it got me into trouble. This trip was one of those latter times.

I had been to Europe only once before, when my father had arranged a summer trip to France and I stayed with the family of an associate of his. How do you find a hotel overseas? I had no idea. Fortunately—at least I thought—a wealthy friend of mine volunteered to have his travel agent make the arrangements. I was so relieved to have things taken care of that I didn't ask about the price; perhaps the fact that I was broke weighed so heavily on me that I just assumed everyone else knew it, too.

$ **Don't forget details you can't afford to ignore.**

When Pat Nelson and I pulled up in a taxi to the front of the Intercontinental Hotel in London, I knew I was in trouble. We were in jeans, tired and sweaty from a ten-hour flight, and had my wheelchair folded up in the trunk, and here was a haughty doorman, dressed like a captain in Admiral Nelson's navy, moving down the line of limousines and Rolls-Royces ahead of us and helping guests with their Louis Vuitton luggage.

Inside, the hotel was palatial, to put it mildly. Our rooms even had canopied beds. In fact, if there was a more expensive place anywhere in the world to lay your head for the night, I have yet to hear of it.

I should have enjoyed the luxury, but I was distracted by wondering how I was going to pay for it. I wasn't the only one worried, and the second day we were there the front desk called to say that the credit limit on my charge card was not high enough to pay for the room. Pat gave them her card, and between the two of us, we were able to incur enough debt to complete our stay.

The London show was held in two enormous showrooms at Earl's Court. It did not take me long to discover that what I had heard was true: in Europe, combining fun and education into one toy was not at all a foreign idea, no pun intended. The London show boasted some delightful and creative games.

Like most industries, the world of toys is actually pretty small, so it wasn't really surprising when I ran into Ted Keiswetter, one of our U.S. suppliers—to whom I happened to owe $25,000. We struck up a conversation, and he asked me where I was staying. I hemmed and hawed and tried to change the subject. I am not a very good liar—but even if I had wanted to lie, I didn't know the names of any cheap places where I could have pretended I was staying. So finally I came out with it: "The Intercontinental."

Ted laughed. "Let's see—am I missing something here? You owe me twenty-five grand and you can still swing a room at the Intercontinental? How come I'm staying in a three-pound-a-night fleabag?"

I was so embarrassed I could hardly speak, but I explained the misunderstanding with the travel agent. Ted was actually very good-humored about it, and I can forgive him if he got a moment's amusement from my discomfiture; probably my wheelchair helped my case, too. We've been great friends and have enjoyed doing business together for twenty years.

❐   ❐   ❐

In Germany, my accommodations were more suited to my station. As it turned out, Ted had the last laugh. Coincidentally, we saw one another while waiting for our bags at the Nuremberg airport. He asked me where I was staying this time. When I told him, he was plenty amused. Little did I know I had a travel agent with a sense of humor; this time she had booked me into a cheap suburban hotel thirty miles outside Nuremberg. Actually, she had no choice, because every bed in Nuremberg is booked a year in advance. Our room was three flights up and there was no elevator, so I begged another American guest, who had a room on the first floor, to switch places with us. He agreed, but he grumbled as he hauled his own suitcase up the stairs.

The first floor may not have had any stairs for me to climb, but it didn't have anything else, either. There was a communal shower and toilet at the end of the hall. The room itself was lit by a fifty-watt bulb, and the bed didn't even have a mattress; it had three cushions that seemed to have been purloined from a neighboring couch. I ended up stuffing my bathrobe and towels into the gaps in an attempt to make it a smoother surface.

Leaving the room didn't help much, either, since Germany in February is freezing cold, and Pat and I had to ride a bus for an hour to reach the toy show.

But when we finally arrived, it was all worthwhile. The Nuremberg toy show is spread out in fifteen or so buildings that were specially built for this annual event. Today I can hit the highlights of the New York show in about three days, but I still can't do justice to Nuremberg in the entire week of its duration.

The competition to get a booth at Nuremberg is fierce because of the expense and because, as big as it is, they run out of space. The variety and quality of the toys matched the size of the show, and even more strikingly than in London, I could see that exactly the kind of toys I wanted were here! But many of these marvelous toys were simply not being brought into the United States by importers.

Clearly I was the woman to change that. But it wasn't going to be so easy. In order for me to buy these toys directly and import them into the United States myself, I had to buy not a few dozen, not even a few hundred, but thousands. The manufacturers who were willing to talk to me at all told me I would still have to go through brokers and importers, which would continue to add to my costs.

The toy manufacturers were not exactly falling in love with me anyway. First, English was less widely used as an international language twenty years ago, and I don't speak German, so communication was difficult. Second, a woman in business was basically unheard of.

I did find something I loved to add to my line: "Unamo," a variation of the card game "Quartet," which in turn is a variation of our popular "Go Fish." In "Unamo," the player has to collect from her opponents a series of four cards that teach a child to avoid accidents. For example, one card in a quartet shows a child peeling a banana, the next shows him eating it, the third shows him throwing the peel on the floor, and the fourth shows someone slipping on it. In addition to lessons about safety, children learn the all-important concept of sequencing. I loved the game and talked myself into spending $15,000 on it. That was the minimum I had to buy in order to import it. Looking back, I think that perhaps I felt the need to buy something in order to justify my trip. Ironically, the toy never caught on back home, although I still think it is a terrific game. What keeps toy selling interesting is that no matter how good your instincts, you never can predict with 100 percent accuracy what will sell. ***Leave room for some errors in judgment, because some will inevitably occur.***

I was so overwhelmed by the choices and so discouraged about ever being able to buy directly from the manufacturers that Unamo was the only product I brought home! But I still chose to see the trip as a success. I learned that there were stimulating educational-and-entertaining toys out there, and I just had to grow big enough to import them directly. Meanwhile, I could still track some of them down by going through middlemen, although that would continue to add to my cost. The trip gave me such an idea for the future that I returned feeling euphoric, my vision renewed.

❐　❏　❐

One of the joys of traveling—even in a wheelchair—is that you have an opportunity to escape from whatever pressures exist at home.

But the pressures wait for you like food going bad in the refrigerator. Ed and Tara picked me up at the airport; Tara was thrilled to see me and blew me kisses from the backseat until we got across the Bay Bridge. Then the acting out began. She started yelling at me about something and kicking the back of my chair.

But I knew that things would quickly resolve themselves with Tara; I was less confident about where I was going to get the $100,000 to pay off my until-now-patient creditors.

Mike Cox thought he might have a solution. While I was gone he had been doing some research and had come across a factoring outfit called Lawrence Heller. They would lend us the money to pay off our vendors and use our inventory as collateral. I was so ecstatic that I didn't pay much attention to the fact that they would also charge us 27½ percent interest or that we would need again to increase our inventory to impractical levels so that we would have enough of it as collateral—so much for careful forecasting—or that they would promptly post a sign on our warehouse announcing to anyone who passed by that Lawrence Heller owned our inventory or even that they would charge us $300 a month for the privilege of posting that sign.

The fact is that I was too naïve to realize that these terms would kill us even faster than angry vendors. ***Some solutions are worse than the problems they are meant to fix.*** We took the money and ran—until May, when the cash-flow monster began to catch up with us again and even someone much more naïve than I could see that we had to do something—and fast.

After Ed and Tara, what I cared most about in my life was Discovery Toys and what we were trying to accomplish. It sure as heck wasn't for the money—not at the rate we were going into debt.

28. Venture Capital? What's That?

A T THE RISK OF SOUNDING presumptuous, I have sometimes dared to imagine that a Higher Power was watching out for me and Discovery Toys. In May, with the Lawrence Heller wolf growling at our door, I received a completely unexpected phone call from a man who described himself as a venture capitalist. For the purpose of our story, let's call him Gary. I had never heard the term *venture capitalist* before, but this didn't strike me as the moment to request a definition. Gary asked if I would be interested in having someone invest in my company. For a moment I was afraid it was one of my more mischievous colleagues playing a practical joke on me.

But as Gary kept talking, it became apparent that this was no joke. His wife, Carol, had been to one of our parties, had spent a fortune on products for their daughter, and had come home raving that we were one of the hottest young companies she had ever seen.

I met Gary a few days later in his office on one of the top floors in the Bank of America building, the second tallest in San Francisco. The sweeping, uninterrupted view of the bay and the Golden Gate Bridge alone was enough to awe me into silence.

I didn't get to stay silent long. Gary was tall and gentlemanly; he served me coffee and held the door for me as we went into a large, airy conference room. I liked Gary immediately. Though not particularly handsome, he had a strong presence and radiated charm—so much so that at first I hardly noticed that he was grilling me as if I were a witness in a particularly grisly murder trial. For three hours he asked me everything there was to ask about my business, my plans, and my personal history.

As intense as it was, I enjoyed this interview. My enthusiasm was as great as it had been the day that Sue and I flew to Los Angeles for the toy show at the Biltmore, so I didn't really feel as though I were being grilled—it was more like an opportunity to tell someone about my mission. Preachers never tire of their subject, and neither did I. Gary's questions showed me that he was a brilliant man, and I love an intellectual challenge.

At the end of the interview, Gary did not commit to investing money, but he promised to be in touch. We shook hands, and I ventured back out into a beautiful San Francisco afternoon. I felt good; I knew I had presented my case well. The air was clear, spring was warming into summer, and there were no signs of the trouble to come.

Three months later, Gary did invest money with us. However, at the last minute he changed his terms. Instead of asking for a 10 percent interest in exchange for a $100,000 investment, he put papers in front of me to sign that gave him a 20 percent ownership in exchange for $90,000. (From the original $100,000 he would deduct a $10,000 "fee.") When I reminded him of his original offer, he replied, "If you were naïve enough to believe that, that's not my problem." I declared that I wouldn't deal with unethical people and stormed out of his office. Soon after I was back; I was just that desperate for cash.

Throughout our relationship, I continued to respect Gary's intelligence, but I certainly had difficulty trusting him after that beginning.

Some years later, we became involved in a costly and bitter legal dispute that even led a judge to comment to me, "Never confuse our legal system with justice." It was one of my harder-earned Learning Moments: ***Look at the whole person, not just at the parts you want to see.***

29. The Rock and the Hard Place

MY FATHER HAS ALWAYS SAID, "If you can't find the road you're looking for, get out your shovel."

That became my philosophy, and it was how Discovery Toys was born. As we've seen, the evolution of my company was not part of a conscious plan; it was more like bad improvisational theater. In retrospect, I can see the forces at work that got us where we are today.

Our line of toys was one of those forces, of course, but only one. Another was that in the late '70s and '80s, large social changes were moving through this country, and the trickle of women who had started returning to work in the mid-'70s was becoming a mighty river.

There were obvious positives to this phenomenon. When my mother got married, the pressure to stay at home full time was so great that exceptions were almost unheard of. Intelligent, energetic women like my own mother could only channel their gifts into charity lunches and bridge games. (She eventually bucked the system, but not until later.)

By the late '70s, women were not just going into teaching and nursing—the underpaid careers traditionally open to women who wanted or needed to work—but were entering law school, business school, and medical school in record numbers; they were training as firemen, policemen, and paramedics. Of course, some fields opened up more easily, and even today, some positions remain difficult for women to penetrate—and even when penetrated, the glass ceiling for women is a reality. It's disheartening for me to observe how few women CEOs head large companies.

Of course I support equal opportunity and equal pay for women. But the downside of the women's movement was that when women were asked what they did, to answer, "I'm a housewife and mother," was very uncool. "Why would you waste your education?" was the question, though often unspoken—because the questioner moved on quickly to talk to someone more interesting. These poor women would even sometimes add "only" in front of "housewife and mother"—as if devoting oneself to raising the next generation were a job to be denigrated! ***Women are sometimes harsh judges of one another.***

It seemed that society went from one unacceptable end of the spectrum to the other equally unacceptable end. Suddenly—it seemed like it happened overnight—staying home with your children and not working was a bad thing! Working is important to me, and I was, if I may say so, ahead of my time when I started my own business so that I could indeed spend as much time with Tara as I wished to. But as years went by, I didn't like to see how many people got knocked over by that swinging pendulum. Why did going to work, especially with young children at home, become the preferred and respected alternative? Since when did a mom who wanted to stay at home with her kids—thus performing a difficult and important job—have something to be embarrassed about? This has got to change. We must give back to motherhood the high status it needs and deserves.

In a perfect world, we would all have choices—to get married or not, to have children or not, to work or not—without pressure to conform to the latest study-of-the-month just released from Study University about what's best for us.

Given the financial realities of many people's lives, that last choice—to work or not to work—isn't always as much of a choice as we might like. But too many families complicate matters further when they turn "wants" into "needs"—and $200-a-pair athletic shoes become a requirement. It bears repeating that the money many women actually take home from their jobs is minimal—childcare, commuting, a career wardrobe, and other extras can wipe out the bulk of one's income.

Women and their families often pay a high price when they hold down demanding jobs while raising their children. Some women get up at 5 A.M. to do laundry so their kids will have something clean to wear to school and to leave time to get breakfast, pack lunches, drive the older kids to school and the baby to day care—and still get to work at nine o'clock. A full day in court, in meetings, at a computer, or maybe even in a police car or fire truck gets her home at six or even seven to find all her children waiting, hungry, cranky, and needing baths and help with homework. If she has a husband's support, some of these needs might be met by ten; by eleven she's falling into bed, exhausted, with only six hours to go before the whole process starts again.

There are many nightmarish variations of this schedule, but the result is often the same: no personal life for mom, kids who simply aren't getting enough attention, a husband with whom one rarely has time to talk, and loads of guilt.

Parenting is a full-time job. Marriage is a full-time job. Working out of the home is a full-time job. In many families, if not most , when mom goes to work, she doesn't relinquish any of her other duties. She ends up not just with one job but with three.

Is it any wonder that so many women are exhausted? Is this what we were fighting for? Is this "liberation"? Does it make any sense to live like this?

It was hard on me, too, but I was able to make it work for several reasons. I had one child, and I was working for myself. I put in a lot of hours, but I was able to do it when I wanted to and could. When Tara was at school or napping, I snatched that free time. I left her with a baby-sitter in the house for a few hours every afternoon, and I did lots of work after she went to bed at night. ***Prioritize, prioritize, prioritize.***

Every woman has to discover her own way. I believe that every woman has a gift that she can turn into income, without the enormous sacrifice she may feel she is making now. Your new path doesn't have to be something exotic or unusual. Perhaps you're a good cook. I would gladly pay someone to deliver nutritious, low-fat, home-made meals to me that I could put in my freezer on a Sunday night and thaw throughout the week. I'd even pick them up! And I know plenty of working women who feel the same.

Maybe you like to knit or embroider or make jewelry. Many boutiques take the work of local artists on consignment. Check the Internet. Maybe you could sell your goods there or network with store owners who might be interested in your product.

Also, the corporate world is increasingly outsourcing many of the jobs it used to do in-house and therefore is looking for freelancers. You may be able to move the job you were doing in an office to your home: graphic design, bookkeeping, public relations, writing, even law. You can take on as many or as few clients as you wish.

I want to paint an accurate picture of the home-based business. First of all, most businesses do have some start-up costs built in, whether it's a new computer, a sewing machine, subscriptions to professional journals, or a drafting table. The good news is that this is all tax-deductible if it is really for your business.

Second—and I want to emphasize this—working at home, or working around your family's schedule, doesn't mean that you don't have to work very hard. Don't fall for a get-rich-quick scheme. There aren't any. If there were, wouldn't everyone be doing them? A number of ECs are making six-figure incomes, but they're not doing it by spending their afternoons watching the soaps. They're setting goals, taking chances, pushing themselves to do things—like calling friends of friends of friends to ask them if they want to be hostesses—that may be uncomfortable at first.

Whether you're an EC or a freelance graphic designer, there's a very big added bonus: Because you are using your gift and living your passion, you are enjoying your work process! Work isn't a dreary necessity, it's a joy. When you are doing something you love, you don't come away tired, you come away energized and fulfilled, and you can have more time for yourself and your family. *Capitalize on your natural talents, and what you do won't feel like work.* You bring this joy back to your children, and they benefit not just from your good mood but from seeing that you—and therefore they—can be in charge of your own life and live that life on your own terms. Being successful as moms may be our number-one goal, but we can only achieve that when our own needs are being met, too.

Caught between the rock of full-time work (incredible pressure, no free time) and the hard place of staying at home all day (no extra income, not much intellectual challenge) is not a good place to be. The balancing act doesn't make for a very good fairy tale. We are continually looking for alternatives. The exciting news is that you have the power within you to create them! You can create a part-time career for yourself!

30. Women Just Like You

BECOMING AN EDUCATIONAL CONSULTANT for Discovery Toys is one of many paths. In my opinion, an EC has the best of many worlds. As an independent contractor, she works for herself. She can determine entirely for herself how much time she wants to put in (subject to the $150 minimum order quota that she must fill each quarter) and she is completely in charge of her schedule. A woman can work as an EC part time, full time, or even as a second part-time job to bring in additional money. (Not all of our ECs are parents, which broadens the spectrum that they bring to Discovery Toys.)

An EC also gets the professional support that only a large organization can provide. We supply the toys, warehouse them, deal with all the vendors, print the catalogs, offer excellent training, and worry about what the product line will be for next year.

We're also able to provide what most large organizations can't: a lot of emotional as well as practical support. The Discovery Toys tradition has been one of abundance. In other words, we all have the attitude that there is plenty to go around: plenty of customers, plenty of product, plenty of ideas. One of the things I disliked about teaching in a traditional classroom was that there was an ethic of hoarding, a sense that people had to keep ideas as well as classroom supplies to themselves. Most teachers I knew were pretty dedicated—or at least they had started that way. The unwieldy bureaucracy that oversaw their efforts did not reward innovation or cooperation or anything, really, except filling out forms and meeting deadlines. It was not an atmosphere in which one easily flourished, and only the most dedicated and resourceful retained their enthusiasm.

At Discovery Toys we do the opposite. We nurture each other's dreams and share all our ideas, from the grandiose to the whimsical. From our regional kickoffs to our national conventions and a thousand ways in between, we cheer each other on and reward our top sellers with applause, awards, and good old-fashioned bonuses. As it says in our EC sourcebook, " . . . while you're in business for yourself, you're not by yourself."

Recognition is important to everyone's self-esteem. Our desire to be acknowledged for our efforts continues throughout our life. It's unfortunate that one of the harder jobs around—running a house and raising a family—is one of the least rewarded. Moms seldom get praised for making the beds well or for cleaning the toilet to a sparkle— or even for raising great kids!

Acknowledge others and ask for acknowledgment for yourself.

Thousands of women—and a few men, too—have been Discovery Toys ECs, and their lives contain many success stories. Of course, you define success for yourself, but I like to see a woman improve the quality of her life with her family. Does an EC have more time to play with her kids than she did when she worked as an administrative assistant, lawyer, educator, or nurse? Can she take her children to doctor's appointments, go to parents' night, or just sit on the couch and snuggle with them?

And does she still get to hang out with grown-ups? Does she even get to bring home some extra money? You bet. Discovery Toys is a perfect way to work part time, but it's far from the only way! You are talented. Use your talent to help you form a vision, and then follow the rest of the steps in this book to start your own business. You may want it to remain a small, home-based business, or you may want to grow it into a conglomerate. That is completely up to you.

ECs range in age from early twenties to mid-sixties and are located in each of the fifty states and Canada. Although we do no screening of any kind, it seems to have evolved naturally that we all share the same values and ethics. And when ECs get together at Discovery Toys conventions and kickoffs, the spirit of camaraderie is invigorating. Here are some of their stories:

Nicky Laman. Nicky was living in Portland, Oregon, pregnant with her first child, when her husband left her. She knew there would be no alimony, no child support. She was working as a dental hygienist, a job which required that she arrive at work by 7:30 A.M. and not return home until 6 P.M. Nicky wanted to nurse her baby when he was born—it was to be a boy, Cameron—and she also didn't want to turn his care over to strangers for what would be something like 75 percent of his waking life.

While she was pregnant, a friend had told her about Discovery Toys, and she was intrigued—until she learned that it would involve giving so-called product parties. "I had never been to a product party and I was proud of it!" she says. "Besides, anything that started in California was suspect."

Nicky dismissed the idea until after Cameron's birth, when she traveled down to the Bay area to show him off. On that trip, the same friend took her to one of our infamous product parties. "On the way over, my stomach was in knots," Nicky says. She was afraid she would be walking into a hard-sell pitch.

Instead, she saw fabulous toys and an informed but non-pushy consultant. Nicky signed up as quickly as she could find a pen, becoming our first EC outside of California.

Back at home in Oregon, Nicky scraped by, often staying in the homes or apartments of friends who were on vacation. Two months after signing on, she returned to the Bay area for an EC training. She describes how she drove up in her VW bug to our modest warehouse— the one I was so proud of—and saw what she remembers as a hand-painted sign. I came out to greet her sporting one of those giant shag haircuts that were popular in the '70s but which look so silly in a lot of family photo albums today. What can I say? The style was a natural for curly hair like mine. But Nicky says, "The light was coming around the edges of your hair, and it almost looked like a halo." And she still tells me how much it meant to her that I had thought to have a Port-a-crib ready for Cameron to use.

At our next convention, Nicky learned that she had been our second top seller for the year to date, even though she had been with us for only a few weeks of that year. The recognition was as important to her as the money.

In 1979, Nicky began recruiting her own team. By this time we had put in place some of our multilevel marketing structure. The structure is complicated and has continually evolved. Back then, by recruiting five new ECs, Nicky became a group manager; as she continued to recruit and as those people recruited in turn, Nicky rose to become first a senior group manager and later a sales director. At one time we thought we would divide the country into regions, as many companies do, but later we decided it would make more sense to let managers have nonexclusive territories. That way she can build a team wherever her heart and her contacts lead her, "from Puerto Rico to Guam," as Nicky puts it.

The important point is that at every level our ECs and managers are motivated to help others succeed. Their success only comes about when they help others. That's entirely unheard of in the corporate world, where climbing the ladder can mean pushing other people out of your way by whatever means necessary. In Discovery Toys, there's no limit to the promotions that are available. Nicky is now a Diamond Sales Director, the highest level in our company. But that doesn't stop any of her colleagues from becoming Diamond Sales Directors, because the title is based on performance; in fact, Nicky is constantly encouraging others to do what she has done.

By the early 1980s, Nicky was earning a six-figure income with us. But that's only part of the story. In 1985, at the age of thirty-nine, Nicky gave birth to her second son, Jordan. This time she chose to be a single mother. She recalls how grateful she was that I was happy for her and supportive throughout the experience—at least after my initial comment when she called to tell me "some great news." I joked, "Tell me anything, Nicky—except that you're pregnant!" I'd stuffed my foot in my mouth big time.

When Jordan was in preschool, he became friends with a little boy named Adam, whose cubby was right next to his. Jordan used to come home and tell Nicky that he wished that Adam, who was one year older, were his brother. Do kids know more about these things than we give them credit for? Maybe. Adam's dad was a single parent, too, and he and Nicky have now been ecstatically married for six years. "It's what your mother always tells you," Nicky says, "about things working out for the best. It's hard to remember when you're going through them, but there came a day when I could thank my first husband for leaving me."

The positive attitudes that are the foundation of Discovery Toys can permeate all areas of a person's life. Not only is Nicky happily married, but her Discovery Toys income has enhanced her family's life with extras she wouldn't have dreamed of years ago, from trips all over the world to the large, beautiful home they now own. But the very best part? "My kids think of me as a stay-at-home mom!"

Nicky's greatest pleasure comes from watching her three sons grow and thrive. Cameron is in college, having just announced that he's going to go for his MBA; he credits watching his mother run her own business as his inspiration. Adam, in the eighth grade now, got straight A's on his report card this year. Jordan is reading at college level and playing premier soccer.

Nicky, in turn, credits the right toys at the right time along the way for helping her sons to develop their full potential. When son Jordan was in third grade, his teacher denigrated his writing skills. Jordan even said to his mother, "She [the teacher] doesn't understand that making mistakes is how you learn!"—a notion he had learned from Discovery Toys via his mother. But at the end of the year he had lost confidence and announced, "I guess I just can't write."

That summer, Nicky spent a lot of time with Jordan in front of the computer with "Storybook Weaver Deluxe®," one of our software products. "The program really developed his imagination. We wrote stories about astronauts traveling through space. Now he's in seventh grade, and he's a fabulous writer."

Nicky's boys have been lucky to have her as a mom. And Discovery Toys has been lucky to have her, too.

Lynn Redlich. Lynn's son, Benjamin, is the ultimate Discovery Toys kid, and the positive effect of this lies at the heart of Lynn's more than twenty years with the company.

I got to know Lynn when we worked together at the Concord Day Care Center, and she accompanied me on some of my first demos in 1976 when I was still borrowing toys from the day-care center. From the beginning she's had the I-can-do-it attitude and the belief in herself that makes so many of our ECs successful. Lynn quickly rose to become a sales director in 1981.

Lynn was already an EC when Benjamin was born in March 1980. He was raised in a home where the very best in educational toys were available. Although he's gotten a bit big for toys, the effects both of having good learning tools and of watching his mom walk the Discovery Toys walk—setting goals, achieving them, and taking responsibility for success or failure—can be seen today. Benjamin is a super-achiever. He got mostly A's in high school, acted in every play the school put on, held various elected offices in the school student government, and even played on the Frisbee team. Now he's attending Reed College.

Lynn loves to tell a couple of stories about Benjamin that took place on an incentive trip in 1996. We hold an incentive trip once a year, always in one of the world's most glamorous locales—the Bahamas, Hawaii, Mexico, and England—to reward ECs and managers, who earn them based on successful performance, a combination of selling toys, recruiting new ECs, and promotion in rank structure. Incentive trips are extravagant affairs, but the ECs deserve it. They've worked hard, and they can really use the days to decompress and have fun—swimming, scuba diving, sunning, and dancing. And there are plenty of activities for the hoards of kids of all ages who come along.

This particular trip was in the Bahamas, where we were all staying in a luxury resort. Benjamin was sixteen, and he soon hooked up with a group of other boys his age and a little older. The resort was very safe, so we could allow these kids a lot of freedom to go off on their own and stay out late.

The first night after spending time with his new friends, Benjamin came back with a dour look. "We were all complaining to each other, Mom," he said. "I have a lot in common with these guys. Do you know that none of us were allowed to have video games or to watch more than half an hour of TV a day? And I don't think any of us have seen a toy gun."

Lynn was startled for a just a moment before she realized that Ben was having a bit of a laugh on her. So when he needled her a little more, saying, "It's tough to be a Discovery Toys kid," she decided to go along with the joke. "That's right," she agreed, "it's very rough being a Discovery Toys kid."

If you've had much exposure to teens, you know that they can be frightening creatures—boys in a different way from girls, but both genders equally so. Parents worry about them particularly when they clump into groups, since their ability to get into trouble seems to increase exponentially with their numbers.

On another night, Benjamin again returned to the hotel room looking troubled. Lynn pressed him about what was wrong, and he finally confessed that he and some of the other kids had done something pretty bad. "I don't know, Mom, we just got carried away."

A lot of things can flit through the mind of the mother of a sixteen-year-old boy, and drugs and sex are usually at the top of the list. Lynn swallowed hard and said, "Benjamin, you've always been able to tell me everything. What happened?"

Benjamin hung his head. "We put some of the lounge chairs in the lagoon."

Lynn was relieved—but not really surprised. She knew Benjamin, after all. It occurred to her that this was what a Discovery Toys kid regarded as high acting out—not shoplifting, not smoking dope, but putting a couple of plastic chairs in the pool at a hotel. The story soon got around the whole resort.

In a 1995 newsletter to her sales team, Lynn wrote, "I have always loved the fact that with Discovery Toys, I have not had to compromise my values and goals as a wife and mother. Since before he was born, Benjamin's needs have always come first in my life."

And this makes Lynn just the kind of woman we have always wanted to have with us.

Teresa Garrison. Teresa, who joined us in 1992 after serving as a hostess for a friend of hers who was an EC, brings a different perspective.

Teresa was a newlywed without any children, and she and her husband had just bought a house. They decided that they would both get additional part-time jobs to earn some of the extra income they would need to fix up their new home. But they were young and liked to be able to take off on short notice, so Teresa's husband, David, was hoping that she could find something to do that wouldn't lock her into any more set hours than she was already working as a software consultant.

It was the beginning of the fall season, and Teresa decided that she would be an Educational Consultant until the end of the year. She did very well. In January, she got the information about our upcoming incentive trip, which was going to be in Hong Kong that year. It occurred to her that if she continued with Discovery Toys throughout 1993, she could earn that free trip—and she did.

On the plane coming home from their Hong Kong adventure the following January, Teresa's husband asked her, "So, what are we going to do to earn next year's trip?"

Two years into her Discovery Toys career, Teresa quit her old day job and turned Discovery Toys into full-time work and a full-time income; she's now a Gold Sales Director.

It isn't just Teresa who is committed to Discovery Toys—her husband is as well. David has always shared Discovery Toys with her, working behind the scenes on what he calls "our" business. He keeps her books, tracks her inventories, makes deliveries, works weekend shows with her, and supports her team when she's out of town. Most of all, he's her biggest fan and best advertisement, and he passes out her card and catalogs whenever he gets a chance.

Teresa has always wanted children, and she and her husband expect to start a family soon. Now she's ready! She already has a successful career that will combine perfectly with motherhood. "I wasn't planning that at the very beginning, but it's worked out as if I had. Not everyone can make a full-time income in their first year, so if you already have kids, you have to give yourself time to make that transition. But I'm already here."

As is usually the case, there's much more than money involved. For the first time, Discovery Toys was work that she cared about. "If you don't wake up in the morning and love what you do, what's the point? I want to know that I'm making a difference."

Teresa knows that she is making a difference with Discovery Toys. One of the things our managers and sales directors do is encourage and support the other women on their team. Teresa describes how she gave a motivational tape to one of her managers, a twenty-six-year-old mother of three. The manager came back to her thrilled with what she had learned: "I've been sabotaging myself because I don't think I'm worth it. I don't have to do that anymore." Teresa was equally thrilled to be part of that young woman's personal growth.

Although she was happily married, Teresa says she "didn't have a dream before Discovery Toys. You're going to grow up, get married, get old, and have grandbabies. That's nice, but isn't there more? The price of not having a dream is so much greater than the price of having one that you have to work for."

Kara Murphy. Kara has seen some of the saddest sights in the world. She had always wanted to make the world a better place for children, so when she got her degree in social work, she became a probation officer, working with parents convicted of child abuse or neglect. Kara's job was to help these parents make their homes safe for their children— children who had been taken away from them and placed in temporary protective custody. It was her job to be an advocate for taking the children away permanently if the parents were unwilling or unable to make those homes safe.

Kara soon learned that when such cases got to court, it was the attorneys and not the social workers who had the real power in determining the outcome. So she decided to go to law school and become one of those attorneys herself. She began prosecuting criminals while still in law school at Notre Dame, having been granted a limited license that allows students to appear in court while under the supervision of a practicing attorney.

Kara met her future husband, Glenn, while she was in law school. When she graduated, they decided to move to Seattle. Kara went to work for the King County prosecutor's office trying juvenile defenders.

In 1997, when Kara and Glenn were expecting their first child, her co-workers teased her that she would hang a sign on her door that said, "Stepped out to deliver baby—back in twenty minutes." In other words, she was a driven career woman; like so many other women, she didn't begin to anticipate how becoming a mother might change her priorities.

Kara went back to work after five and a half months. Fortunately, she was able to share her job with another prosecutor and work only three days a week. Still, she found herself under great pressure. More than once in the middle of a trial she'd receive a call from her son's daycare center telling her that he was sick and that she needed to come get him. Were she to leave immediately, a mistrial would be declared—so she would have to wait until court recessed for lunch and rush her son over to a friend's house before returning to court with her sick baby weighing heavily on her mind.

In the fall of 1997, Kara hosted a Discovery Toys party and bought two different starter kits with no intention of doing anything more than keeping the toys for her son. Kara's husband couldn't help but wonder, though, how a party that was supposed to lead to free toys ended up with Kara writing a check. Kara's EC told her that if she sold $2,000 in toys and recruited one new EC in her first eight weeks that the entire cost of the kit would be returned to her. Kara had already signed up a friend, and within a few weeks she sold $2,300 in toys.

For the next nine months, Kara was a part-time EC, working just during her days off from the prosecutor's office. At this low-key pace, she sold $33,000 in toys. When she talked to mothers interested in buying Discovery Toys products, she would say, "You can pay me now or pay me later—because I've seen the results of parents not playing with their kids."

In September 1998, Kara went to the Discovery Toys convention in Anaheim. She arrived with some reluctance, still considering herself a prosecutor, not an EC. She thought that our conventions were for the die-hard, rah-rah indoctrinaires.

But at the convention she heard the children of ECs get up and speak about what it meant to them to have their mothers available to them throughout their lives—to cheer them on at soccer and to be home when they were sick. Kara started to weep. "Here I was so focused on affecting the lives of other children when the biggest opportunity to affect the life of a child was right in front of me in the eyes of my beautiful son."

Kara called her husband from the airport to tell him that she was quitting the prosecutor's office. When she returned to Seattle, she went to her boss to tell him the same. He looked her up and down, and then, knowing that firms specializing in criminal defense often try to lure prosecutors into private practice, he asked dryly, "Who got you?"

"My son," Kara replied.

You might say that Kara is still a driven career woman. She is a senior manager, goes on incentive trips, and earns almost as much as she did with the prosecutor's office. "But it feels like I'm earning more because I've cut down on my expenses so much by working from home," she says. If you ask her, though, what she's most proud of, she will not mention those things—she will tell you the story of Julie Shumacher, another woman who recently joined her Discovery Toys team: "This is a woman who has two small daughters, ages three and a half and two and a half. The younger one has medical problems that require frequent trips to the hospital and at least three therapy appointments a week. This mother would give anything in the world to spend more time with her daughters. It's going to happen. She's been promoted to group manager already. And when she quits her full-time job and gets to work from home, I will have experienced my biggest Discovery Toys success of all—I'll have given another mother the gift of time with her children."

⊓   ❑   ⊓

Discovery Toys isn't for everyone. I'm sometimes dismayed to come across someone who thinks that this is like one of those get-rich-quick schemes you see promoted at 3 A.M. on a cable channel with a double-digit number. These women may be confusing the notion of working flexible hours with not working. The beauty of a career with Discovery Toys is that you can choose to work when you want, full or part time, and set your own goals. But that doesn't mean you don't have to put in any hours!

All of our ECs have had to work hard for their dreams, because that's the way dreams get realized. But there's no greater joy in life than accomplishing something you've worked hard for.

Direct selling may be for you, even if Discovery Toys isn't. If you think you might want to sell clothes, knives, pots and pans, or vitamins, call the Direct Selling Association at (202) 293-5760 for ways to connect with the product that's right for you.

Many women have made grand accomplishments that reach far into the corners of their own and others' lives.

31. Tips for Starting a Home-Based Business

I'T'S NO SECRET that I'm passionately in favor of moms working at home. For me, work was a necessity—but being available to my daughter was an even bigger necessity. Being my own boss enabled me to do both.

Starting a business is a big step—but it's one you approach more easily by breaking that really big step down into a series of smaller steps:

Choose a business. This is where you connect your vision statement with your areas of strength. Everyone has a marketable talent. If you don't think you do, I say it's simply that you haven't looked closely enough at your gifts and your passions! The possibilities for home-based businesses are endless. We discussed this briefly in chapter 29, but it needs expansion because enjoying your life is so important.

One obvious choice is to take what you were doing for an established company and start doing it on your own, whether it's technical writing or interior decorating or financial planning.

But perhaps one of the reasons you want to work at home is to make a change from what you were doing. Then you must ask yourself,

What do I most want to do? Where is there a need I can fill? Be creative! Some people will gladly pay someone to come over and help them organize their closets. (If you're good at that, you have a rare and precious gift indeed.) What about baking specialty cakes? I even knew one lady who was available to write long, intricate poems for special occasions. Perhaps you have a talent for helping people accessorize their wardrobes cheaply. The list is infinite. Your choice of business may be much less unusual. All that matters is that it's something you want to do.

Entrepreneur or co-trepreneur? You can start something entirely new, or you can plug into an existing business and work independently within it, thereby being what I call a *co-trepreneur.* Discovery Toys provides this kind of an opportunity; essentially you work for yourself while still gleaning many of the benefits of working for a large corporation. Being a real-estate agent is another example of the many co-trepreneurships available.

Working with a partner. Many great businesses start in the kitchen when one woman says to her friend, "Hey, everyone loves these brownies/ placemats/quilts that we're making—why don't we start selling them?"

There are compelling advantages to working with a partner/ friend. Entrepreneurship can be lonely, but with a partner you have someone with whom to share both the joys and the burdens. You do need to complement each other in at least some ways. Perhaps you are better at marketing while your partner/friend is better at keeping track of the budget.

If you want to ensure that your partner stays your friend, you both should do some serious planning at the outset. Discuss every possible scenario you can think of in advance, and agree who has the final say in different areas. Do some research. There are books available on partnerships and partnership agreements. Put the agreement in writing and have an attorney look at it.

Among the issues you should attempt to resolve in advance are sick leave, vacations, childcare, and work hours. (How will you feel when your partner calls you for the third time that month and says she can't make a meeting, and you have to cover for her?) Perhaps most important, when you come to a disagreement —and you most certainly will—who makes the final call?

One of the most important contingencies you must prepare for is what happens if and when one partner wants to leave the business. You must also recognize the possibility that one of you could die.

No matter how you plan, there will be unanticipated events and issues. Be prepared to continue to negotiate with each other, and realize that these negotiations can be long and stressful. Ironically, the more successful the business, the more stress there's likely to be between you.

Define success. I am absolutely stunned at how many people overlook the crucial step of defining what success means to them—but not at all surprised by the trouble it gets them into. In fact, I believe that many a home business fails because the person launching it was unclear about what would make her feel successful. How can you achieve a goal if you don't know what it is? I've heard women in Discovery Toys state that they can't make enough money. I always ask them, "How much money had you planned on earning?" To my astonishment, only about one in ten has an answer. The inevitable next question is, "How do you know you aren't making enough money if you don't know what 'enough' is?"

A definition of success is not just about money. It can be about personal growth, recognition, or mission. Perhaps your goal is to receive a college degree in six years. If you think about the effort involved in receiving your bachelor's, you may never start. But if you take one course a semester, eventually you will have your diploma.

Your definition of success must be reevaluated from time to time. You may find it has changed. Today, perhaps, enough money for basic necessities is your greatest concern. In a few years, with that goal met, it may be more about getting your product or service known on a larger scale so you can buy a boat or save for your daughter's college education.

Determine the hours that you will put in. Launching a home-based business is about taking dreams and making them reality. And the reality is that you have to work. You get to work for yourself, and you get to choose when—but you do have to work! Sadly, all too many people imagine that working at home means making a few phone calls while the baby naps.

The beauty of your own business is that you can decide how much you want to work. But you must realize that your income and other successes will be commensurate with the time you put in. You cannot replace the full-time income that you earned in forty or more hours a week if you work only four hours a week. Many women start a home-based business because they don't want to work a forty-hour week anymore. That's fine. In fact, the amount you earn per hour may increase dramatically over time; eventually you may be able to make more working part time than you did full time. But any business takes time to build up. The Small Business Administration (SBA) in Washington, D.C., publishes inexpensive and very good booklets on starting a small business. I've listed their phone number and Web site in the resources at the end of this book.

Make sure you have childcare for the hours you are working. Depending on the nature of your business and the age and temperament of your children, they will probably enjoy becoming involved in your work to some extent. But you are likely to need childcare, too. Your colleagues/clients/customers will not take you seriously if you are jiggling a baby on your lap while you discuss their taxes/new brochure/lawsuit. The world views you as you view yourself. Are you a mom playing "office" or a businesswoman choosing to work from home?

In chapter 15, we look at childcare options in depth, which may include your husband, your mom, a friend, or someone you hire. For the purpose of your business, childcare must be reliable and predictable. No one is going to take you very seriously if you schedule an appointment with the proviso, "This all depends on my husband getting home in time."

Network. There's a double purpose to networking: support for you and marketing for your business.

Make a list of all the people you know. Set the goal of putting down at least a hundred names. This will encourage you to think really hard not only about your friends but also about your many acquaintances. Include your kids' school, your church or synagogue, your friends, neighbors, relatives, hairdresser, people you've met at the gym, and so on. You'll be amazed at how long the list is. Call everyone up and share the good news: You're in business! You're available to cut hair at people's houses, to do their grocery shopping, to make Halloween costumes for their kids. Whether or not the particular person you call is in the market for your services at the moment, always ask for referrals to other people who might be interested in what you are offering. It's much easier to call a stranger when you can start the conversation by saying, "Hi, my name is Lane. Jenny North suggested I call you."

I do realize that making any phone call can be very frightening. Before you lift the receiver, remind yourself of why you are so passionate about what you have to offer and how lucky someone will be to have the opportunity to use your products or services. When you find someone at home, make sure to smile while you talk. If necessary, put a mirror by the phone to remind yourself. A smile will entirely change your tone of voice! Remember that whether or not someone wants what you are offering at that moment or at all is not a reflection on you personally; it is simply a statement of their particular needs.

Pass out your business card. Post a flyer at the Laundromat. How will people come to you if they don't even know you're there? Most of all, don't be shy. Remember, we're all insecure. You may feel hesitant to ask a friend to host a Discovery Toys party because you don't want to impose. And she may feel hurt if you don't ask!

Ask for support. People love to help! Even the most radical entrepreneurs don't do it all alone. In my case, the Direct Selling Association has been a source of tremendous information and assistance. Look in the phone book for organizations that are relevant to your endeavor. Talk to your local chamber of commerce. These days, almost every organization has an 800 number. Get on the Internet. Attend one meeting of any group that you think you might want to join and get on the appropriate mailing lists. Ask your friends if they know anyone doing something related to your new business. If they don't know someone directly, they're likely to know someone who knows someone. This is "power networking"—going beyond your own circle.

Create an office—don't play office. You need to have a physical space that is your own for a number of reasons. It helps keep you organized—who wants to be searching all over the house for files?—and it helps you transition from work to home life. When you walk out of your home office and close the door behind you, you are back home and can think about making dinner for your kids rather than about work.

Of equal importance is the message that an office area sends to the rest of your family. If your husband comes home and sees paperwork spread all over the dining-room table and piled on the chairs, not only may he become annoyed, but he's also not likely to take you seriously—not to mention that some three-year-old might find your letters and her pink marker an irresistible combination.

If you have an extra room in your house or apartment, you're in luck. In these days of runaway housing costs, many of us don't have that luxury. Your space doesn't have to be large, it just has to be yours. Place a desk—or even a card table!—in the corner of the quietest room and put a screen around it. Park your car in the street and take over the garage. Or, since eating with young children is usually an informal affair, maybe that dining-room table can be your permanent office. Your husband won't be annoyed at the mess if the room is off-limits to him anyway.

"Playing office" also means doing non-revenue-generating activities. Organizing your files for the third time may make you feel like you are a businessperson, but it won't bring in a dollar in revenue. Picking up the phone and/or hitting the street in order to market your business will. Finally, make sure you keep careful records of the money you spend both for tax-deduction purposes and so you know where you stand financially at all times. And please, don't spend money on unnecessary things. An automatic stapler, pens in five colors, and a brand-new metal file cabinet are probably not necessary.

I'm not suggesting you want to or will end up as the CEO of a multinational corporation. But who knows? Mrs. Fields started because she liked to bake cookies, and I just wanted to get my daughter some good educational toys.

32. Enlisting Your Family's Support

Launching a business may be scary for you, but it's scary for your family, too. Will there be microwaved pizza for dinner every night from now on? Will you be using expressions like "no-brainer" and "forecast" and "P and L (profit and loss) statements"? Your family's perceptions and expectations of you may change, and change of any kind gives almost everyone a good scare—not least of all you!

Your family is probably your highest priority; they are probably one of the main reasons you want to go into business for yourself in the first place. If you have been a stay-at-home mom, starting a business may mean that you won't be as available to satisfy your family's every whim. That can be a good thing—maybe it's time your six-year-old started pouring her own juice.

If you've been working full time, going into business will mean that you have more time for your family—but not full time. Remember, you will still have a job to do, but you can set your own hours.

In either case, of course, you need and want your family's support for your new venture. Here's how to get it:

Approach your husband with a business plan. In this day and age, do you really need your husband's permission to start a business?

It's not a question of permission—it's a question of communication and a question of your partnership. Your husband or partner, hopefully, is sharing his major decisions with you as well.

Abundant research indicates that men and women think different from one another: men put more emphasis on logic, numbers, and facts, while women tend to be more intuitive and interested in the emotional side of the equation.

Although generalizations like this one can be dangerous if we take them too seriously, I believe that the genders do have different ways of thinking, so I suggest using a strategy that is businesslike and logical rather than emotional. Your husband or significant other is likely to appreciate it and in turn give you the support you would like more easily. Approach him the same way that you'd secure approval if you wanted to launch a new project while working within a company:

❑ State the objective clearly.

❑ Outline the benefits for your boss and for the company (or your significant other and family).

❑ List the resources necessary to ensure that the project will be completed.

❑ Include an impact study showing how different departments would be affected.

❑ Construct time frames for completion of various stages of the project.

❑ Listen to, clarify, and respond to any objections.

If you were to make this kind of presentation at work, you would sit down with the necessary parties and calmly discuss your plans. If your management showed any reluctance or doubted the viability of the plan, it's unlikely that you would yell, cry, or even walk away angry. Probably you would explore their concerns; perhaps they're resisting because of other problems in the company or because you have not painted a clear picture of your project. You would most likely listen to them carefully and ask any questions you had in order to ensure that your next go-around answered them. And you would, of course, do any further research needed.

Why not treat your partner at home the same way? I don't know about you, but I don't always transfer my work skills to my home. Instead of going to your husband and whining about your long commute and your psycho boss—or, if you're a stay-at-home mom, complaining that a whole day without adult conversation has you on the edge of going postal—and then telling him that you must make a change starting today, why not make him a thorough business proposal instead?

Since we all fear change, the "I need to make a change today" approach is likely to have him become defensive immediately. "Oh my gosh," he'll think. "I don't have any idea what this means, but I'm afraid I won't like it." It's a natural human reaction to any unknown change. The most likely outcome will be a nasty argument instead of an open and important conversation between two partners.

Let's illustrate these principles in detail.

Objective: "I want to start a home-based business making healthy meals for other working women. I plan to start September 15, and I think I can make $500 per week.

Benefits: Great marketing always starts by fulfilling a customer's needs. In this case, your husband is your first customer. What needs of his can you fill by starting a home-based business? State the benefits to him: "By leaving my full-time job, I won't be as tired at night, and we can have more time together. Since I'll be cooking for others, there'll be a lot more home-cooked meals, and I'll have the dog walked by the time you come home so you won't have to do it." You know his hot buttons; see how many you can push. But be sincere! You must believe that this opportunity will make a positive difference for him.

Next, paint a picture of the benefits that this will bring to the two of you as a couple. (Threatening him with divorce if he doesn't cooperate is not normally considered a great benefit.)

Finally—and potentially, most powerfully—point out the many benefits that will accrue to your children: you will have more time to help with homework, to read to them, to work on the computer, to go to the library, and to help them pursue their after-school interests such as soccer or music. Remind your husband or partner that a parent is a child's most important teacher and that by having more time available, you are ensuring that your children receive the best possible head start in life.

If you are a single mom, of course, your first customers are your children. If you can sell them on your idea, it will be much easier to forge ahead. Adapt these steps as practical.

Necessary resources: Show your husband or partner your income goals and your basic plan to achieve them. Explain that you will be sharing your progress with him as you move toward those goals. Show him what you were actually earning by working and how you plan to cut costs until your income grows. (See chapter 14, "Working May Cost More Than You Think.")

Next, outline what your expected start-up costs will be and how you intend to find the capital. There is no doubt that starting any business will require some capital, though it may be as little as a couple of hundred dollars.

Outlining expected expenses is critical to gaining his support. No one likes financial surprises, and leaving him in the dark on this point may lead him to imagine that your expenses will be much higher than what will actually be necessary. If you expect to need any nonfinancial resources, such as turning the guest bedroom into your office, now is the time to bring them up.

Impact study: Your impact study is an opportune place to reiterate to your husband or partner the benefits of your business and also to introduce any additional help you will need from him and ways the children can possibly be of help. In Discovery Toys, for example, many demos are held at night, after dad is home to take care of the kids. If you haven't gone out at night before by yourself, this will have a real impact on him. Depending on your husband or partner, this may be fine with him—don't forget to point out that there is no baby-sitting cost—or you may need to assure him that dinner will be ready, the kids will be bathed, and their homework will be finished before you go out. Take things a step at a time. Don't push for an immediate answer. If your husband is the type who likes to mull things over, give him a chance. He may surprise you if he doesn't feel pushed into a corner. If necessary, reassure him that you already feel he is a big help and that you aren't taking this additional requested support for granted. (This is not being manipulative. Everybody needs to be appreciated. The more we tell others what we appreciate about their behavior, the more likely they are to continue that behavior.) Although he may not believe it at that moment, I can assure you that by having to take care of the kids by himself, he will become closer to them and someday will look back and be glad he took that important step.

Time frame: Outline how long you think it will take for you to start making money and what your projected expenses will be before you make a profit. Unless you work a hundred hours a day and already know everything there is to know about your business, you will undoubtedly lose some money in the beginning. If you don't "play office" and if you spend money only on income-generating activities, you can shorten this period considerably. Of course, what your actual expenses will be is at best an educated guess. Assure your husband that if the plan does not work the way you have outlined it, you will discuss it with him. This way he won't feel afraid that money is going to just disappear somehow and he'll be responsible for finding more.

Objections: Listening to objections is perhaps the most important part of ensuring that your family will support you in your new business. In any situation where you wish to influence someone, it's important to remember that an objection is not a no—it is simply a request for further information. Don't try to persuade your husband, or anyone else who you're trying to influence, that you are right. You'll never be able to persuade them if they still want or need additional information.

When an objection is raised, we tend to become defensive or try to ignore it by talking around the issue. When you have internalized the fact that an objection is simply a disguised request for further information, it will change your entire life. Listen to others' concerns with an open mind and acknowledge them. Be sure that you are truly listening to both the words and the melody, not framing answers in your mind while others are talking. To ensure that you have completely understood, repeat back each concern as they come up, using your own words, before you reply for yourself.

For example, a customer's common objection to hosting a Discovery Toys demonstration is, "I just don't have enough friends." Usually this means, "Will you, the EC, really want to come if I have only four or five people there?" Alternatively, your husband may express an objection by saying, "I hear that 90 percent of new businesses fail. You have no experience. Why should you succeed?" Do not immediately interpret this response as his lack of faith in you. Actually, he may be feeling anxious about taking over a larger share of the family's financial support. When you understand that, you can respond by reiterating how much money you realistically expect to earn and in what time frame.

Imagine if your husband came home one day and announced, "Darling, I'm so excited. I've quit my job! I'm going to start my own business baking cookies. I don't have any idea exactly how to start, and I have no idea if I can make any money, but I know it's going to be a great adventure!" How supportive do you think you would be?

As your discussion proceeds, let him know that you respect and value his input and hope that he'll contribute his insights to your business. You will note how much I am emphasizing this repeat-then-respond process. That's because it's a crucial one in so many situations. It forces you to listen to your husband's real concerns instead of formulating an answer in your head while he talks. Then you will truly be answering his real objection, not what you think he may be saying. This will feel awkward at first. Don't give up! With time, it will become second nature to you.

If you don't know the answer to a question he asks, don't guess. Tell him that in fact you hadn't thought of that particular issue and you appreciate his helpful thought process. You can either continue to discuss it further with him or tell him you will get back to him by such-and-such a date and then follow up.

By following the plan outlined above, you are becoming a true businessperson. By showing your husband the benefits for him, for you as a couple, and for your children, you have set the stage for him to hear what you have to say. By truly hearing his concerns and repeating them back for clarity, you are understanding his issues. By explaining the resources required and giving him the information he has requested, likely through an objection, you are taking away any mystery. Most people are very reasonable if they see some benefit for themselves and/or feel their partner understands their concerns. You are much more likely to get support for your proposal as long as the resource requirements, timeline, and likely profit make sense.

It is unlikely that you will agree on everything. Marriage is based on compromise. But by using this approach, you can have a calm, open, and rational conversation. We can do anything by ourselves, but it is a lot easier and more fun if our husbands or significant others are behind or next to us.

Allay your children's fears. I believe that children are not here to support us, we are here to support them. One of the first things you need to do when you start your new business is to sit down with your children and talk to them about it.

As with any subject—and especially weighty ones such as a death in the family, a move, or a job change—you need to gear your talk to what your child can understand. A one-year-old may only be able to appreciate that this is Mommy's briefcase and Mommy's computer, while a teenager may be able to give you advice about financing. Your teen will certainly be able to use the Internet to help you do research.

Your children, every bit as much as your husband, need to know what the benefits will be for them in this change. If you are going to be home more, that will be the most obvious benefit. If you've been home full time and now you are going to be gone for a few hours every day or so, you need to find a different benefit. For example, is there something important they have been saving for? Depending on their ages and personalities and depending on what you choose to do, you may be able to include them in your business. They can earn money from you by stuffing envelopes, passing out flyers, stamping catalogs, answering the phone professionally and making a note of who called, or making deliveries. We have ECs with ten-year-old children who occasionally do dynamite demos of their favorite products right alongside their moms.

Don't burden your child with more than he needs to know. For example, don't say, "Mommy's making $40,000 at her job now, and she will be making less for a while. We will all have to tighten our belts." Money is out of their control, and all that will do is frighten them. What they do need to hear is your assurance that while there may be a few changes, their needs will always come first and the changes are going to be exciting.

Get your children involved. Elsewhere I've pointed out how important it is to be professional about your work. Hearing your kids fight in the background while you talk on the phone is not going to build confidence in your clients! But there's more to it than that. When you spend time with your children, give them your undivided attention. And when you're at work, focus on work. Otherwise, the work doesn't get done and your kids don't get what they need either.

But that doesn't mean your children can't feel a part of what you're doing. One of my fondest memories is of listening to my dad talk about his work at the end of the day. Let your kids see your office space—even if playing with your computer is a no-no—and show them see what you're selling or what you've made, or let them taste what you've cooked up. Let them get a sense of what you're doing when you're not there. My daughter loved the idea that she was a Discovery Toys "toy tester." This wasn't just an honorary title. Her opinion, expressed by how often she wanted to play with a specific product, was very important to me.

Nothing brings better results than doing something fulfilling. If you love what you do, you will be happier and all the more able to give of yourself. The more you can give without feeling empty in return, the happier everyone will be. Life is a constant spiral. Keep yours turning in an up direction!

33. The Year of the Black Hole

A S CEO OF DISCOVERY TOYS, some days I felt like one of those inflatable clowns that just keeps bouncing back up no matter how hard you hit them. Other days I just felt like a punching bag. No matter what I felt, I was there almost every day, and in part because of that, it looked as though Discovery Toys was going to succeed. *Just showing up is at least 60 percent of the reason you succeed.*

Entrepreneurs as a group are determined and visionary; our minds run at about twenty-five ideas per minute. We are driven by our dream. We have a product that must reach the marketplace, a service that must be offered. "Build a better mousetrap and the world will beat a path to your door" runs the old expression. But it only seems that way. In actuality, the man or woman who has built the better mousetrap will do the path-beating, knocking on every door in town and showing off the new invention, exclaiming, "Try it—you'll see how much better it is! I'll give you your money back if you don't agree!" Our mousetraps, or in my case, our toys and our desire for every parent to have them, are the fire that drives us ahead.

Ironically, the very qualities that drive an entrepreneur to succeed can later cause her to fail. At the beginning, it's a good thing we want to do everything, because we have to do everything. Most start-up companies can't afford to hire professional help. I was no different. In the first few years of Discovery Toys, I had gathered around me a number of friends and friends of friends. Like me, they were dedicated, and we were all having a lot of fun together in spite of the crises that were our daily bread.

As the business grew, though, I began to face the fact that it had outgrown the skills of some of these wonderful people. *The people we like to have as friends and the people we need in business aren't always the same.* By the end of 1982, we had reached the $10 million mark. That's a lot of Boomerings® and Marbleworks®! But as I looked around the company, I saw an ex-preschool teacher, a carpenter, and an old friend, but not one professional manager—including me. Meanwhile, we had accounting, forecasting, and purchasing systems to build, an entire computer program to design from scratch, and a twenty-thousand-square-foot warehouse to manage.

I had reached what is a crucial turning point in many small businesses. It's the point at which many hard-working entrepreneurs lose their businesses because they can't manage every aspect of them and they can't bring themselves to delegate. *Once your product has proven its viability, the most important aspect of growing a business is gathering the right mix of people around you—people who are smarter and more experienced than you are.*

I realized that in order for my business to succeed, I needed to let some of my staff go. This triggered a personal crisis. I was and am deeply indebted to the people who came on board early. How on earth could I possibly ask them to leave? But I knew deep in my heart that it wouldn't do any of us any good if I lost the business. If that were to happen, thousands of people would be hurt. I had to find people with the professional experience that could grow Discovery Toys to the next level.

In January 1983, my venture capitalist, Gary, called me. He pressed me to hire a COO—a chief operations officer—to handle the day-to-day operations, freeing me to concentrate on product and the field. Gary planted serious seeds of self-doubt concerning my ability to continue to run the business on my own. I already knew that the business had outgrown the talents of my staff. I concluded that he must be right—it must have outgrown mine as well.

My Discovery Toys experience has been a string of firsts, and this was the first time I had to hunt for and hire a COO. I didn't have any idea what to look for in such an individual or even how to begin the search.

I did know that I was more than ready to turn over some of the day-to-day tasks. I was beyond exhausted. For five years I had been a mom and had tried to keep a marriage together while shoehorning Discovery Toys into every free hour. In some ways, though, what was so exhausting was not the time commitment but the learning curve, which was so steep and slippery that I sometimes felt like I was climbing a glass mountain. In five years, I had had to learn virtually everything there was to learn about direct sales and small-business practices, from accounting to purchasing to running a warehouse and everything in between—as well as manufacturing. And I'd learned it all not in the safety of a classroom but in a real-life situation where any mistake could blow up the lab. I had a finite capacity to absorb it all.

One of my newest staff members had come from another direct-selling company, and she highly recommended a man whom I will not identify by his real name. Let's just call him Jonathan. He looked great on paper. Jonathan had helped, or so he told me, a troubled direct-sales company execute a miraculous turnaround. Encouraged by this background, falling in love with his silver tongue, and trusting the word of my staff member, I didn't bother to check Jonathan's references; worse yet, I gave him free rein. After all, if I had to watch his every move, that would defeat the purpose of getting help in the first place. *Delegation does not necessarily mean giving up authority. It means setting appropriate parameters in which an employee can freely function.*

With Jonathan on board, I confess that I was tempted to let him perform the unpleasant task of firing some of the management staff, including—it still hurts me to say—Mike Cox and Pat Nelson. I was physically ill at the thought of letting them go and didn't sleep for days. I weighed not only the future of Discovery Toys into the balance but my responsibility to our field—the thousands of women who were out there selling our toys and relying on us for part or all of their income. *Sometimes you have to weigh the good of the many against the needs of the few.*

In the end, I accepted that I could not delegate this difficult chore, and in one of the saddest times of my career, I fired several good human beings. *Don't ever shirk difficult decisions, no matter how painful. It's your job to take full responsibility for making tough decisions.* Due entirely to Mike, we are still great friends to this day!

I let Jonathan replace my staff with his own people, which turned out to be a huge mistake but one that I wouldn't recognize for nine months. What I did know right away was that I didn't like Jonathan's people very much. They were arrogant and seemed to feel they knew it all—traits often symptomatic of people who know very little. *Trust your intuition about people. If you feel in your gut that something is wrong, it probably is.* But for the time being I was determined to stay out of internal affairs and concentrate on building the organization on the outside.

As 1983 dragged on, I began to notice that we were showing slightly bigger losses than the previous year. I had grown accustomed to the losses themselves, because that was the nature of the toy-business beast: We would post losses through August and then start to see things turn around in September, when we would begin to turn a modest profit. The previous year had been our best yet. Not only did we have $10 million in sales, but by the end of the year we had earned a 15 percent pretax profit.

At the very beginning of September 1983, things still seemed on track. We were expecting to increase our annual sales to $25 million. And I was enjoying my new role in the company. Hiring a COO had helped free me to spend more time with the field, which I adored, and to pursue my newest idea, which was developing our own toys. Attending the Nuremberg show early that year, I was no longer as dazzled as I had once been. It had become clear to me that we needed to become proactive. We had already imported many of the truly great toys available. Most of our suppliers were small companies without large research-and-development budgets. They were able to introduce only a small number of new toys each year, and most of those I didn't like. Within a few years we would run out of new toys to import, and I wanted to be ready for that day.

When I received our September financial statements, though, they drove all other thoughts from my mind. By now I could actually read the financial statements, and instead of showing the small profit I expected, I saw that we had losses of $200,000. Every expense was way off the chart: office supplies, warehouse supplies, equipment, payroll.

I confronted Jonathan, who was pretty slick with his response and managed to convince me that he had everything under control. I desperately wanted to believe him, so I did. I decided that I would at least give it another month. ***Don't suddenly become blind and deaf to information you don't want to know about—it will inevitably come back to bite you.***

Then, on November 17, the October financials landed on my desk. I hated myself for deciding to go along with Jonathan. We were close to $20 million in sales—but our losses now totaled $800,000. Worse yet, it looked as though the losses would only continue to build. In short, we would soon be bankrupt.

I went home. Ed met me at the door, and I told him that we were out of business. Then, for the first and only time in my life, I went straight to my room without saying hello or even goodnight to Tara. I got into bed and lay perfectly still under the blankets. It was a night reminiscent of my near-fatal car accident. My head certainly hurt just as badly as it had then, maybe worse, and the shock was even greater!

Morning came. I woke up and tried to summon the energy to get out of bed. I was enraged at Jonathan, but I was also angry with myself, an emotion that drained what little strength I had left. How had I let an outsider run away with my business? ***Anger is rarely productive. Let it go as best you can and move on.***

Could I fight yet another battle? I didn't want to. I wanted to quit. There was little hope of surviving this catastrophe, so why not give up now and spare myself the pain, the humiliation, and most of all, the incredible effort that would inevitably lead nowhere anyway?

I pulled the covers over my head. It was dark and warm and safe there, and for the moment, I had no intention of leaving. In the darkness, I imagined myself going to my last Discovery Toys convention. I visualized myself standing up in front of five thousand Educational Consultants and saying, "I'm out of here. I know I told you that you could support yourselves at home and change the world one child at a time, but I'm sorry. I'm simply too tired to continue. I quit!"

I also asked myself, would I be lying in bed if my daughter were dying? I don't think so. I'd have to die first. I certainly wouldn't be home, feeling sorry for myself. I'd be in her hospital room, doing anything I could to keep her alive. Discovery Toys was not Tara, but it was in many ways like a second child to me.

While considering my alternatives, it had occurred to me that I could sell the company. By selling, I could make up the losses and walk away with a substantial personal gain. Yet once again, the realization of what Discovery Toys meant to me revitalized me. I was not about to give up on it now. ***There are rewards in life that are far more important than money.***

Suddenly I was up and getting dressed in my one and only good business suit. I spent a little more time than usual on my makeup, the better to look the part of a woman in complete control. That morning, it was not a facade. It was the only time in my career that I have not gotten sick before I had to fire someone; in fact, I felt just fine about doing it.

I entered the building, marched into Jonathan's office without knocking, and announced, "Jonathan, you're fired."

"I beg your pardon?" he asked.

"You're fired," I repeated through clenched teeth. "Get out of the building and I'll talk to you later when I've calmed down enough to ask just exactly what has happened to this company."

For once Jonathan did not try to convince me that all was well; I was on to him and he knew it. He collected a few things and left. We changed the locks the next day.

34. Life or Death

A FTER FIRING JONATHAN, the next thing I did was call my executive staff together for an emergency meeting. I had an image of
myself in my mind as the strong CEO taking back the reins of the company, leaving no doubt in anyone's mind as to our certain future. But
when I started to describe what had happened and what we were up
against, I broke down in tears.

Perhaps this expression of genuine emotion was more effective
than toughing it out would have been, although I was embarrassed.
The important thing is that the whole staff committed to staying with
me and helping to work out the problem as best we could.
*Believe in the humanity of those around you. People may care
more than they demonstrate.*

I couldn't imagine how we had lost so much money so fast,
and the truth is that I still don't know what happened to that money. If
we had commissioned an intensive and expensive audit, we might have
been able to uncover some answers, but I knew intuitively that we had
neither the time nor the money to worry about it. We had to
move on. *In a crisis, don't waste your energy trying to find out
who was at fault; move forward to correct the situation.*

We all walked around in a daze the rest of the season. Without a COO, and about to be sucked into an $800,000 quicksand pit, we simply tried to cut costs wherever we could and hoped we could reduce our losses in what was left of our crucial fourth quarter.

Then I got a call from our loan officer at Bank of America. "We've decided not to renew your loan in January," he told me casually, as if mentioning that it might rain that weekend. "You need working capital, and we don't care to be in that business." What business were they in? I wondered. The loan was for $1 million, and I could no sooner repay it than I could fly to the moon on gossamer wings. *In the world of finance, always expect the unexpected.*

❐   ❑   ❐

The story of how we had gotten this loan is itself worth telling. In the fall of 1980, we applied to the Small Business Administration for a loan, which was to be underwritten by Bank of America. But by May 1981, it still had not been approved.

Once again, I was cash-desperate. Sound familiar? What I should have done was to get more venture capital. But I had felt so betrayed by my one experience with a venture capitalist that I was afraid to get involved with another one. In retrospect, this was probably a mistake. *Don't let bad experiences with one person prejudice you against others.*

Ron, one of my board members, accompanied me to a branch of Bank of America in Berkeley, where we met with the loan officer assigned to our account. He was very kind but told us there was nothing he could do. Until the SBA approved the loan, he couldn't give us the OK.

"Well," I replied, "I'm sorry to hear that, but I'm not leaving this room until you approve the loan." Naturally, he didn't believe me. I'm not sure I believed it myself. A few hours later, when I was still sitting in his conference room, he came and told me again that there was nothing he could do and that he really needed me to leave. "We may have to call security," he said.

"Call the Coast Guard if you want," I said. "I'm not leaving. And if you do have me thrown out, I'll take my story right to the press." I left the loan officer to imagine how the story would look in the newspapers: a woman, a small-business owner, thrown out in the street by the big bad corporation.

He didn't have me thrown out. In fact, he was very nice; he simply couldn't approve our loan without SBA approval. But as the day went by, Ron and I stayed in the conference room, cleaning out a pizza box, reading magazines, and wondering how this was going to end.

At the end of the workday, the loan officer reappeared. "You know," he sighed, "I'm a Catholic, and after work I'm going straight to church to light candles for both of us. If the bank auditors come in and see what I've done before I hear from the SBA, I'm going to lose my job. But meanwhile, all right, I'll give you the money."

One month later, the SBA finally did approve the loan. I was very relieved for both of us.

❐   ❑   ❐

Now, about a year and a half later, I had been planning to ask Bank of America not only to extend the loan but also to increase it. Instead, they were pulling out entirely. Our performance that year must have troubled them, but the abrupt timing has always disturbed me. It was the first time we had shown a loss. Why didn't they at least want to look at our plans for the future? Whatever their reason, once again, our best course of action was simply to move forward.

My next step was to call my accounting firm, which was one of what was then the Big Eight—the eight largest, most reputable accounting firms in the country. This particular accounting firm had always been a source of good advice and referrals in the past; we were probably their smallest client, but they treated us very well. I explained the situation and begged for help. (I'm never too proud to beg, if necessary.) I knew that what I was asking of them was way above and beyond any call of duty—and probably impossible: find me the smartest, most experienced, most trustworthy financial manager in the country and have him in my office yesterday. I didn't care if he or she could consult with me for only a short time. I was desperate.

Two days later a woman from the firm called me back. "I've found someone terrific," she told me, "but he's retired and only available to consult with you for two weeks." That would be the absolute longest—two weeks.

Two days after that a man named Jim Hitt walked into my office and saved my company. ***When what you are doing is important and ethical and you express your need from your heart, people can appear in your life in just the nick of time.*** Jim was an elegant man in his late fifties with a beautiful head of silver hair and perfect posture. His résumé was even more impressive than his appearance. He had been chief financial officer of American President Lines, one of the world's largest shipping companies, for much of his career. Jim was one of the kindest and most skilled people with whom I have ever worked. If he had not walked into my office that December, Discovery Toys would undoubtedly have closed its doors in 1983.

Jim could read financial statements the way a literary critic reads a novel, interpreting not only the numbers but understanding the scenarios that had generated them. He confirmed my original instinct, though, when he told me, "I don't know what went wrong here, and it does look quite strange. However, it will cost us too much to find out. We're just going to move ahead." If ever there was a time to cut our losses—literally—this was it.

The Higher Power that has helped me along the way also has a sense of humor—or at least likes to test mine. In mid-November our "computer" system bombed out. I put *computer* in quotes because by today's standards, the Basic 4 system that we were using was like stone tablets and a chisel.

Even in 1983, the Basic 4 wasn't cutting edge, but it was doing what we needed it to do—basic accounting, keeping a record of our orders, issuing pick slips for the warehouse, and paying our field—until it stopped doing even that.

I called Basic 4 headquarters in New York City three or four times a day for ten days. Finally I got the president of the company on the phone and told him, "All I want to know is, on what flight will the person who is coming out to fix this machine arrive? If he is not here within twenty-four hours, you will receive a $40 million lawsuit for ruining our entire business." I was so sad that the only way I could get the help we needed and deserved was by threatening to file a lawsuit, which I would have done if necessary.

They did send out a technician, and he held our poor little computer's hand while it died a peaceful death. By the time we caught up with the ten days lost in November, we couldn't deliver a single December order. Is it any wonder we at Discovery Toys call 1983 the Year of the Black Hole?

By all rights, Discovery Toys should have followed the Basic 4 to the grave. But with Jim now at my side, I was ready to fight to the very end.

Security Pacific Bank—which, ironically, was later swallowed by Bank of America—had been courting us as clients for a couple of years. Their president had even been to see us, but I had felt too loyal to Bank of America to switch. Now I called the president of Security Pacific and told him that I had become thoroughly tired of the turnover of loan officers at our current bank. (What I really meant was the turnover of the loan itself.) A Security Pacific executive and loan officer were in our office the next day.

Jim and I gave them our audited financials from the previous year—the year we had made so much money. When she asked about the current year, Jim said, "You really have to see the twelve-month cycle in order to get the complete picture." After some further discussion in bankese, a language that Jim spoke fluently, Jim asked them for a $2 million long-term line of credit. They quickly and eagerly came back with tentative approval of the loan pending a review, of course, of our current end-of-year statement. At that point, Jim explained that we had a minor problem: We had actually lost about $700,000 that year. Before they fainted, he pulled out some chairs and we all sat down. We explained our plans to put things right. We knew we couldn't sell our way out of our problems. We had to contain costs. Jim was eloquent and sincere, and he "forgot" to inform Security Pacific that he was planning to stay only through Christmas of that year. On December 23, Security Pacific approved our loan. I imagine their confidence was due partly to our previous track record, partly to the fact that Jim was so experienced, and perhaps partly even to the Christmas spirit. Whatever the reason, it was certainly one of the best holiday gifts I had ever received and a happy enough ending to what I hoped was really, this time, for sure, the worst year of my career.

35. Rattles to Riches

A MUCH MORE POSITIVE SIDE to 1983 deserves equal billing; as I've already mentioned, it was also the year in which I began fulfilling a long-held dream: developing our own toys.

The gift of being able to invent toys grew out of my vocation as a creative educator. If I may say so, it's a nice gift to have. I had been having fantasies of creating my own toys ever since I became a mother. **Give yourself the chance to discover your own gifts.**

There were practical reasons for me to start thinking about it again now. I knew that the day was soon going to come when we would run out of new products. Of course, the need to keep putting new toys in our catalog was not to satisfy children's desires; rather, it was to catch the eye of parents and the interest of our Educational Consultants. The two-year-old who is ready for her first Giant Pegboard® doesn't know that it was in our catalog before she was born. But Americans are newness junkies, and there are a lot of companies ready to feed their habit. The desire for novelty runs so deep in us that I have never wanted to buck the trend.

We decided to start with two projects: a super-lightweight rattle—no more bumps on the head—and a crib mobile. We brainstormed a lot of ideas for the rattle, which we decided should look like an animal. We discarded kittens, puppies, and bears in favor of a monkey, thinking it would be the most original. It certainly was. When the prototypes popped out of the mold, they looked like ugly and scary gorillas. Our catalog copy could have read, "Give your baby her very first trauma!" We were $20,000 into this project at this point, and it was tempting to try to sell the little monster. We certainly couldn't afford to lose $20,000. But we threw away the mold. Our philosophy was, and is, that we will never send our customers merchandise that is anything less than exceptional. *Compromising your values for short-term gain will result in long-term loss.*

After several years of trial and error, we finally developed the rattle that we still sell today in an updated version. Necessity was at least a kissing cousin of this invention. At the time, we could not afford to manufacture a busy box—a box with multiple activities that attaches to the side of a crib—so we thought, why not make a rattle that functions like a portable busy box? The eventual result was our Jungle Rattle™ activity center. It was the size of a rattle and easy to hold, but it was also equipped with rings to twirl, textures to feel, sounds to make, and animals to teethe on. At its center was a smiling face, because that's what babies first react to.

Like the rattle, the crib mobile had been a pet idea of mine for some years. Most crib mobiles to this day have delightful critters that look great to parents but don't look like anything to the baby lying under them.

Our original design for the crib mobile involved flat cardboard disks that faced down so the baby could see them. But we were unable to manufacture the fixture on which the mobile would hang, so we ended up with a design that required the buyer to string the disks himself— with string that usually arrived hopelessly tangled. Once put together, the baby could see the wonderful patterns—but unfortunately, since the clamp that attached the mobile to the crib never quite worked either, no baby I know of got to enjoy it. All in all, it was a complete disaster. None of these problems stopped me. I realized that developing toys was far more difficult than I had first thought, and I needed to find the right sort of engineering help.

Even the simplest of toys takes eighteen months to two years to go from conception to market. My mobile has broken all records for having the longest toy-development time in history. Sixteen years later, we finally introduced the mobile of my dreams: the Picture Perfect Melody Mobile™—four brightly colored fiber-filled squares hanging down, facing the baby. In each square there are windows in which the parents can insert photos of mom, dad, or grandparents—or the cards we provide, which are printed in various colors, patterns, and pictures geared to stimulate the baby at various stages of visual development. ***Time and persistence will eventually lead to the results you want.***

Once a baby is able to raise himself up in the crib, mobiles become dangerous. So we designed the squares to detach from the mobile and to link to our Boomerings®—plastic connecting rings—to become tooth-proof portable picture frames. Oh, yes, the mobile also functions as a music box, which plays a piece by Mozart—whose music, some research has suggested, particularly aids in brain development. We like to say that it's a multimedia toy for babies, and we feel it was well worth the wait. I'm proud to say that our mobile just won the National Parenting Award.

Early on in my toy development, I came up with Measure Up!® cups. The uses of these simple stacking cups grow right along with the baby to include many opportunities for developing pre-math and then actual math skills. The cups are numbered, and they're volumetrically correct—the contents of cups number one and two fill cup number three, or cup number one will fill cup number three, three times. I was desperate to help my dyslexic daughter understand the concepts underlying math. Math is an abstract concept, and most children can only learn it by using various manipulatives to help them take the abstract into the concrete. I knew that Tara needed better learning tools, that she had to become physically involved. By pouring water or sand into the different cups and experiencing the concept over and over, she finally got it. What a rewarding experience for both of us when her face lit up with understanding! Like many of our products, babies can start using Measure Up!® cups at eighteen months and still be enjoying other uses for them in first grade.

Naturally, not all our products are intended to span such a wide age group. But a really terrific product transcends the lust for the new and doesn't have to be replaced; nevertheless, we're constantly refining our products, even our classics.

Today, 90 percent of the products in our catalog are either our own designs or toys we have co-developed with other designers and manufacturers. Our innovative toys form the basis of our reputation. They've given a lot of happy learning hours to thousands and thousands of families.

You learn through your mistakes, although sometimes you pay what seems like a few trillion dollars for your education. You might say that in our early years as toy designers, we invested in the finest education available! Another example is the snap blocks we developed. They were fabulous; each block had snap fittings on all sides so kids could literally snap them together as they built. The prototypes we received from Taiwan were perfect, the picture in the catalog was sensational, and our ECs were already taking orders for them. We could hardly wait for our first shipment.

Finally the big day arrived. Many of the staff joined me to watch the truck back up to our warehouse, so eager were we to see the first of what we just knew was going to be our biggest seller of the season.

One of the crew, a big burly fellow, opened the back of the truck to start unloading the blocks. He literally passed out. The rest of us ran for cover. The stink was catastrophic. Our colorful snap blocks had been painted with a fish-oil-based paint that simply would not dry. I mean "would not dry" as in "never dries, not ever, no matter what you do." We tried putting the blocks out in the California sun for several days. No luck. You could have held a blow dryer on one of those little beauties for two years and the smell would still asphyxiate you.

It would have been funny except for one minor detail. Back then we hadn't heard of letters of credit, a financial instrument that banks have devised to protect both buyer and seller. We had paid for the blocks when they were put on the boat in Taiwan. We buried our money and the blocks together in a hazardous-waste area. ***Know when you can trust and when you need to use caution.***

◻   ◻   ◻

Through all of these discouraging blunders, I could have said to myself, "Lane, you are too stupid and inexperienced to design your own toys, or for that matter, to run a business. Give up."

I could have said it back in 1977 when no one wanted to rent me a warehouse because I was a woman and they figured I would go out of business and stick them with unpaid rent. I could have said it back in 1979 when I went to the Nuremberg toy show and no one wanted to sell me anything because they thought my company was too small.

No one enjoys setbacks. But some people, when they see an obstacle, tell themselves that it's all over, that there's no way to get around the fact that their path is blocked. My friend Rosemary uses the analogy of water-thinking versus rock-thinking. When a boulder rolls into a creek, the water can't flow straight ahead as it did before. But it can always find its way around or over the boulder—and eventually even through it. A rock-thinker says, "Now that the boulder is here,

I have to stop." A water-thinker says, "I wonder which option I'll choose for moving forward?" ***Obstacles can be seen as stimulating chal-*** ***lenges to solve, as opportunities to learn something new, to do*** ***something different and better.***

Are there things in your own life that you've tried once and then never attempted again because you failed the first time? Watch a baby who hasn't learned the failure trap. Watch her as she learns to walk. She lets go of the edge of the couch, lurches forward, and falls to the floor. Two days go by and she's still eating carpet. But she keeps trying. Every time she lets go of the couch she gets half an inch farther. Another week and she's stomping around the living room as if she owns the place.

If babies took the attitude toward failure that most adults do, we would all still be lying in our cribs. We wouldn't even have any toys to keep us company in those cribs because no one would risk developing them. It's a risky enterprise, and even today we have some big expensive failures. There's no question in my mind that some failures are necessary steps to success.

Jan Ruhe, one of our Diamond Sales Directors, has a valuable lesson to share. The conventional wisdom in our business and in marketing in general is that regardless of what you are offering, you have to ask ten people before you get a yes. So, for example, an EC might have to call ten prospects before someone agrees to host a party. Jan says that every time someone says no to her, instead of thinking, "Poor me, nobody likes me. I'll never get anywhere," she thinks, "Fantastic! I'm one no closer to my yes!" No wonder she's a Diamond Sales Director!

The greatest fear of all is rejection. Achieving your goals isn't just about working harder; it's about taking chances. Maybe you aren't recruiting as many team members or booking as many demos as you would like because you're shy about putting your message across. All this means is that you need more practice or that you haven't really internalized your mission. If you believe in what you have to offer, why wouldn't others want to know about it?

Maybe you aren't working on your novel very much because you're afraid of quitting your day job. Maybe you're afraid of applying to college or graduate school or applying for another job because you're afraid of the disappointment you'll feel if you are rejected.

We all fear rejection; we all fear finding out that we're not good enough. But you have choices: you can let the fear stop you, or you can acknowledge that you feel it and move forward. If you are going to be a businessperson, it is critically important that you realize that rejection is not personal. It is not about you. Perhaps the college had too many applicants from your state and ended up accepting students from your state by date of application but never told you so. Or perhaps the admissions office filled available places first with people who did not need any financial help, and you do. There are thousands of excellent colleges in this country, and many of them would be happy to have you.

Perhaps you didn't get the first job you applied for because they already had an in-house candidate but went through the motions of searching anyway. Or perhaps you reminded the interviewer of his ex-wife! That's why you have to apply to a large number of colleges and jobs. Business according to Lane: "Fear of rejection is the number-one reason most people fail in small businesses." (Lack of cash is a pretty close second.)

If you find that your fear of rejection—or any other fears—chronically get in your way and that you're just not making the progress you want, I urge you to seek professional help. Don't wait—and don't let shame or embarrassment or some unstated fear stop you. Not getting the help you need can lead to failure. Seeking help can lead to success.

36. Nine Really Simple Steps to Achieving Success

TOO OFTEN I SEE PEOPLE fantasizing vaguely about success, doing nothing to pursue it, and then, as time goes by, telling themselves, "I guess I'm a failure" or "I guess I'm not like those other (successful) people." This drives me crazy, and it also breaks my heart.

Of course you can be successful! It doesn't have to be the stuff of other people's lives. Success requires that you first define the term for yourself. Then you need the vision, the desire, the persistence, and the plan to achieve it—on your terms.

Keep a success notebook. Choose a clothbound, unlined journal or an inexpensive spiral notebook from the five-and-dime—whatever you feel most comfortable with. Keep a record of your actions, step-by-step, from defining success to recording and monitoring your progress.

Define success for yourself. We don't all want to work at the same job, drive the same car, or marry the same person. If asked, each of us would define success differently. And yet, how often, if indeed ever, do we take the time to ask ourselves what our definition is. Maybe it's as simple as having enough money to pay for food and shelter. Maybe it's being able to afford braces or summer camp for your children. Maybe it's having the time to take a field trip with your child's class. Maybe it's earning $100,000 per year and having a BMW in the garage.

Goals may or may not be linked to money; success can lie in recognition, knowledge, or personal growth. Frequently, what we want more than anything is simply to have more time for ourselves or for our families. Imagine the sheer luxury of taking a bath for as long as you like, with soap bubbles and a great novel and absolutely nobody interrupting!

Our definition of success is also likely to change over time. Having our first child often drastically affects our definition of success, which may become more about filling our children's needs. It doesn't matter what your definition of success is as long as it's yours and not what your mother thinks it should be or what your neighbor believes. The only value judgment to apply here is, "Is this really what I want?"

Most entrepreneurs will tell you that they did not start their businesses for money. In our society, money is a report card and, to some degree, a source of power. However, once our basic needs are met, there is no such thing as enough money. No matter how much they earn, most Americans live slightly above their income. There is always someone who has a bigger house than you do, who takes fancier vacations, or who owns more toys.

Establish a concrete goal. "To be rich" or "to be famous" are perfectly acceptable goals, but you must translate them into something concrete. What does "being rich" mean to you? Ask ten people, and each one will name a different figure. What does "being famous" mean? Do you want to be in your local newspaper or on the cover of *Time* magazine? Decide what price you are willing to pay to achieve success, and I don't mean financially. No one becomes rich or famous without giving up many other parts of their lives.

A goal has to have clear definition, an expected result, and a time-line—for example, "I want to be a Diamond Sales Director in Discovery Toys, earning a six-figure income, by June 30 of next year."

Perhaps your goal is to quit your full-time job by May of this year while managing the family finances so that no additional debt is incurred. Once you have established a clear goal, you have to carefully plan the steps required to achieve it. In this example, the steps required may mean cutting certain expenses. Perhaps you have to do something radical like selling your house and moving to an apartment or renting a smaller house. Maybe it means cutting out all fast food and going to fewer movies. Maybe it requires every member of the family to cut their spending by 20 percent. That may sound like a horrific amount until you identify just what that 20 percent means in real dollars. Maybe you spend that much on coffee drinks each month without even realizing it, and identifying the amount may give you the incentive to finally kick the caffeine habit. Maybe together you and your husband can resume doing household chores such as cleaning and yard work instead of hiring others to do it.

There are many creative ways to cut spending that do not necessarily have to radically alter your lifestyle. You will never achieve a spending cut, however, without a carefully articulated and specific plan that you all agree on.

If your goal is not both clear and specific, you set yourself up for failure. If you say, "I want to be thinner," how do you know when you've achieved your goal? On the other hand, if you state, "I will (*not* want to) lose twenty pounds in four months," you know exactly what success looks like. Now you can start making a plan to achieve it. If you say, "I will earn the Discovery Toys incentive trip to Paris this year," you've made a clear statement, and the requirements are laid out for you. Since there are many different ways to achieve them, however, you absolutely must put together your own personal plan.

Break your goals into small, attainable steps. Let's say your goal is to write a novel. It's a big, intimidating project. If you sit down Monday morning to write your best-seller, no matter how motivated and talented you are, you may soon find yourself lost.

Work backwards from your goal and see how you can divide getting there into manageable chunks. You want to complete your novel in one year. You estimate your novel will be four hundred pages and that you will write two drafts. This means you have twenty-six weeks in which to write each draft. Working five days a week means you have to write approximately three pages a day. That seems much more manageable than staring hopelessly at four hundred blank pages, doesn't it?

Similarly, let's say you want to promote to group manager at Discovery Toys in two months. Although you can do it just by your own sales, it is much easier to promote having other members on your team. Let's say you want to add five people to your team in two months. Using that good marketing rule of thumb, you have to talk to ten people to get one yes. This means you'll need to talk to fifty people in two months in order to add those five new ECs. That breaks down to twenty-five per month, or less than one person per day.

The importance of breaking your goal down into daily activities is readily apparent. Talking to fifty people is really scary and may very well intimidate you into never getting started, but talking to one person each day is easy. Even shy people could face their fear and call one person a day. By the time she has made ten or twenty calls, her fear will have completely passed. Writing a four-hundred-page novel is a potentially paralyzing thought, but writing three pages a day seems doable. Goals such as these set you up for success. Instead of wistfully pronouncing, "Someday I'd like to be a group manager" or "Someday I'd like to write a novel," you are making measurable progress toward your long-term goal, and there is no doubt you will achieve it.

Write down your monthly, weekly, and daily goals in your success notebook. Then follow through, follow through, and follow through.

Evaluate your progress. On the last day of each month, review your goal for that month. If you have met or exceeded it, fabulous. You should feel successful and know that you're making exactly the right progress.

If you didn't meet your goal, do not beat yourself up. Reevaluate. You have choices. You can (1) set yourself the goal of catching up—after a month it's still possible—or (2) decide that you don't want to meet the original goal and realign it to match what you are willing to do.

Let's go back to the goal of losing twenty pounds in four months. That means losing five pounds a month, or a little more than a pound a week. But suppose that after the first month, you've lost only two pounds. You can say, "OK, I have to diet more strictly next month and lose eight pounds in order to stay on goal," or you can say, "If this is what it takes to lose two pounds, that's OK, because it's all I'm willing to do. So I'm going to change my goal and take ten months to lose twenty pounds."

Does that make you a failure? Of course not! You are a success for losing two pounds and for moving toward your goal. But all too often people say, "I didn't meet my goal. I guess I can't do it after all." Not only do they feel like failures, but they're likely to put back on the two pounds—and more.

That's why it's so crucial to evaluate your progress. Depending on what you are trying to accomplish, you may want to evaluate weekly, or if necessary, especially in the beginning, even daily, to make sure you're on track.

Find a buddy. No one is totally self-motivated in every area all the time—so don't make that another thing to beat yourself up about. The challenge of staying motivated is the reason that people go to church, therapy, or Weight Watchers each week. Witness the value of daily AA meetings to the recovering alcoholic. I once read, somewhere, that human beings can stay motivated for only about forty-eight hours. I can believe it!

You need to find support for yourself, too. I recommend that you pair off with a buddy to form a mini-support team. Your buddy should have goals of her own so that you'll be able to support each other and remind each other of your goals and planned activities through frequent reviews of your individual progress. Ask one another questions such as, "Have you accomplished what you set out to do today? If not, what is standing in your way—other than you? What can you do to ensure that those issues do not continue to occur? Do you need to realign your goal?" Be sure to help one another find solutions to your challenges, and celebrate your successes. At the end of each month, be totally honest with yourself and your buddy. If you haven't met your plans, how are you going to catch up? What is standing in your way? How can you resolve the problem? Letting yourself get behind more than one month will likely mean you can't meet your yearly plan. It's much easier to catch up for one month's shortfall than for six months. Nothing will let you fail more quickly than believing you will catch up next month and next month and next month. Whether her goals are in the same or a different arena, your buddy should be upbeat and support you totally. Please, don't let yourself fall into the trap of finding a "victim" buddy. Instead of achieving, you will spend the time explaining and accepting one another's excuses. Checking in on one another several times a week—even if for just five constructive, problem-solving minutes— will keep your motivation high.

Explore other ways of getting support. There are likely to be networking groups in your area, or on the Internet, of people in the same or related fields. Some women join groups like Women Business Owners or the Junior League. Writers often join writers' groups; law students have study groups; psychologists have supervision groups. Don't expect to do all this on your own.

Beware of spending way too much time on the Internet. It is easy to feel that three hours in a chat room sharing ideas with others is an income-producing activity. Information exchange can be helpful, but it needs to be brief and businesslike. All the ideas in the world won't make you a penny if you don't put them into action. If you want to chat, by all means have a ball—just not during your business hours!

Make a treasure map. Get a poster board or use butcher paper—anything that gives you a large canvas. Make a simple map to show where your progress is today and where you want to be at the end of the year (or at any other ending point you choose). You can do this project on your own, with a buddy, or with a larger group. It can be an enjoyable way to get your children involved in your success. Use colored markers to make drawings and/or cut pictures from magazines to illustrate your goals. Along the map, post clear monthly markers with the expected outcome.

For example, if you are working for the Discovery Toys incentive trip to Paris, you might draw a picture of the Seine River and separate it into twelve months. Alongside each month's label, paste or draw pictures of various places in Paris representing the twelve months of the year. Perhaps a plane could be the starting mark and the Eiffel Tower the end point. Each month you or your family can color in a piece of the river representing that month's goal. Are you entitled to fill in that entire month's piece of the river? Are you falling short, or are you ahead? Not only will this be a fun way to keep track of your progress, but it is also an excellent visual for your kids to help them really start understanding setting and achieving goals. Maybe they too have something they want to achieve and can create their own treasure map next to yours. When you or your child don't make a goal, you can all talk about what needs to be done next month to make up the difference. In the months that you or your child are on target or even ahead, have a family celebration.

Start a success file. Another motivational tool is the success file, which you should keep right alongside your success notebook. Whenever you receive any positive written feedback—a letter from a satisfied customer or an award—put it in your file or on your wall. When you need a reminder of how terrific you are—and we all need those reminders from time to time—take out the file and review it.

Stretch your goals further. Once you become realistic about your goal, you don't beat yourself up when you don't get exactly where you planned—you either make up the difference or retool your goal.

And once you are clear about working toward your goal and getting comfortable with the activities involved, it may be time to push yourself—just a bit. Maybe you can do a little more than you thought you could. If you are willing to experience some discomfort or even fear, you can set a new standard for yourself.

Suppose you've recruited two new team members each month or booked four demos—can you make it three team members or six demos a month? What would that do to your monthly income? Would it also promote you to a new level? If you're writing three pages of your novel every day, can you make it four?

I hope you will take these steps. I have taught Success Seminars for Discovery Toys ECs hundreds of times over the years. The results can be phenomenal. I want you to be a success, too.

37. The Circle of Life

I N J A N U A R Y 1 9 8 4 , Jim Hitt was due to leave Discovery Toys. I pleaded with him not to go, and he reluctantly agreed to stay with us until tax time.

Jim had done so much for me and for Discovery Toys that I never could have repaid him. Our next hurdle was not really taxes—after our disastrous year, we didn't have to pay any. Instead, I needed Jim to navigate us through the then-uncharted seas of a new computer system.

When you walk into Office Depot today and see the wide aisles of personal computers lined up, ready to do your bidding at a keystroke, it's hard to remember back a mere fifteen years ago when computers were about ten times the size, a hundred times slower, and arrived without Windows, Quicken, or anything loaded on them. Back in the prehistoric days, there was no prepackaged business software available. Rather, companies like mine had to hire a team of experts, whom we couldn't afford, to write a computer program, line by line, for our machine, which we also couldn't afford. In those days, the simplest and smallest computer cost $27,000 and couldn't do a tenth of what an $800 machine does today.

Working on this project was all the fun you might imagine. One program would finally get up and running only to refuse to "talk" to the other programs. No sooner was that fixed than we discovered that the "fix" had caused three other programs to crash. We had a dozen techies actually sleeping on mattresses in the office, working all night, and eating pizza for dinner at 1 A.M. At one point, the head of our department got so stressed that he locked himself in his office and wouldn't come out for two days. We finally lured him out with a box of jelly doughnuts. He still wasn't smiling, but he went back to work.

April turned to May, May to September. Jim got us through all of it. He cajoled, promised, yelled, and held hands. Although many years later we had computer problems that surpassed my wildest nightmares, for now, thanks to Jim, we had a system up and running in time for the fourth quarter. And this despite IBM telling us it absolutely couldn't be done. *There is nothing you can't accomplish in the business world. It's simply a matter of time, money, and persistence.*

Jim was also a patient mentor to me; I learned more from him than I can record. He was always kind and gentle and never made me feel stupid. He encouraged me to question everything and taught me that there is no such thing as a silly question. He was also constantly encouraging me by telling me how smart I was and how quickly I picked things up. *No matter how successful one becomes, one always appreciates positive reinforcement.*

Jim saved me yet again in May 1984. It was time for our annual cash-flow crunch. This year it was made far worse because the computer problem was costing us far more than we had anticipated. In short, we were short by $1 million.

Early in the year a gentleman named Doug Rumberger had joined us as COO; he was a brilliant referral from my dear friend and business coach Chris Hahn. Doug had started a medical-equipment company and had recently sold it for a vast sum of money. Like Jim, he had retired, but like a lot of gifted businessmen, he soon got bored without a few daily fires to put out.

Doug was a fabulous COO, and we were lucky to have him. He was also, shall we say, a little bit tight with money. Actually, he made Jack Benny look like a compulsive spender—this in spite of being a millionaire many times over. We teased him about it unmercifully, and he always took it in good fun.

Jim and Doug had become close friends. When Jim realized that we were not going to make it without an infusion of cash—which the bank wouldn't give us—he marched into Doug's office and said, "You need to lend Discovery Toys a million dollars." And Doug did! This was nothing short of miraculous, since getting Doug to buy bananas when they weren't on sale was a challenge. I am forever grateful to him—but I don't think he would have done it for anyone but Jim. *Miracles do happen. Sometimes they occur when you think life can't get any worse.*

❒　　❑　　❒

Another good fortune that befell me in 1984 was having Mike Clark join Discovery Toys.

We were looking for a purchasing agent. Rich Newton, who was running our warehouse, suggested that I meet with Mike Clark, who had been Rich's boss at Sunset Designs, a company that sold needlecraft kits to hundreds of small retailers. Mike and I set up an interview, but nothing you could call an interview ever happened—it was more like a reunion. I felt as though I had known Mike forever. I don't really believe in past lives, but if I have lived before, whenever and wherever it was, Mike must have been in the hut or tent or igloo next door.

Mike and I made the perfect team. I need to think out loud because I'm an auditory learner and process information best by hearing. I have a tendency to wander around the office tossing out ideas:

"We should have the convention in Waikiki." But the next day it's "Did I say Waikiki? I've thought about it and I think Rio would be better this year . . . How about New Orleans?" Meanwhile, a staff member has already printed up a brochure promising everyone Waikiki. "Hawaii?" I'd ask? "Where did you ever get that idea?" I had forgotten that I'd even mentioned it. *It is critically important that you understand different learning styles and can identify how people, including yourself, learn. It's especially important to understand the learning styles of your children in order to avoid serious homework battles.*

As you can imagine, this sort of thinking out loud isn't easy on everyone else. In this case, being president of the company worked against me, too, because people assumed that I already knew what I wanted before I even spoke. *People perceive you as the role you play, not necessarily as yourself.*

Mike intuitively understood my process. He was the perfect foil for my ideas and always sensed exactly when they were ready to go to press, as it were. He was a brilliant thinker in areas complementary to mine, and he loved a good open debate, as do I. Among hundreds of other things, he was a genius at follow-up, my severest weakness. After years, I finally had someone with whom I could share the twenty-five ideas that exploded in my head like kernels of popcorn each minute. Mike very sensibly wouldn't make a move until he heard my idea repeated for the third time. Then he'd decide I was getting serious. If needed, he would do the research to see if the project was viable and come back to me with facts and figures. Should we add fifteen or twenty toys to our line this season? Did it make sense to expand into Canada or Mexico? When the Hostess Plan needed to be changed and updated, he figured out the complicated math involved in the change so we didn't lose money.

Sometimes he'd say, "You're the boss and it's your decision, but I don't think you are going to want to make that particular decision, and here is why." Actually, as soon as I heard the words "You're the boss," I knew my idea was doomed. He was truly a partner, and I loved him dearly. Together we were much stronger than either of us alone.

A big problem for most CEOs is that few if any staff ever tell them the truth, especially if the staff thinks the CEO doesn't want to hear it. *Encourage your staff to be honest with you, but realize that complete frankness will be rare.* I found that my staff often thought I already knew about a specific issue that was bothering them and wasn't doing anything about it because I didn't care to. In reality, I was frequently the last one to hear about the problem, if indeed I ever did. *The larger the organization, the more filters the information passes through before it reaches the final decision maker. Often a good idea is killed long before it even gets there.* From the first day, Mike always shared exactly what he thought. I learned to trust him 100 percent because of his honesty and intelligence.

In the late fall of 1984, Doug Rumberger decided to leave Discovery Toys. Our parting was amicable. Doug wanted to go back into medical equipment, a field he knew well and in which he'd been extremely successful. Mike stepped in to become our COO, and I look upon his tenure as the Golden Age of Discovery Toys. But like all golden ages, it was not destined to last forever.

❐   ❐   ❐

In early January 1985, I was in a hotel room in Miami, the day before our annual incentive trip. This year's trip would be on a cruise ship in the Bahamas, and it would be in two parts because so many ECs had earned this trip that we couldn't get all of them and their families onto one ship, so we booked two consecutive cruises.

The phone rang, and I assumed it was Ed or one of my parents, who would be joining me for the first trip. But it was Marianne, comptroller of our company. She was crying, and I heard her say, "Jim's gone."

Gone where? I thought, in that illogical way you do at such times.

Jim had some pain in early December that was first diagnosed as a back problem. Several weeks after receiving that diagnosis, he had a mild heart attack, and he was then told that he could return to work by mid-January.

Instead, I learned from Marianne that Jim had had another heart attack. This time it was fatal. He was fifty-nine years old.

I was numb with shock. That evening, at our first gathering as a group on the cruise ship, I went to the podium where I planned to share with the field that our beloved CFO had passed away. Although I was by now a polished public speaker and never at a loss for words, I was completely unable to talk. It was a blessing that my parents had joined me for this trip. As he has so often, my father came to my aid at this crucial time. He took the microphone, made the announcement, and told everyone that if they were to truly honor Jim's memory, they were to have a wonderful cruise because it was the only way he would have wanted it. While I knew that Dad was 100 percent right, I remember that cruise as the worst trip of my life.

Jim hadn't really wanted to come out of retirement. He had come for two weeks and stayed because he loved me, the mission of Discovery Toys, and our field. He literally gave the last year of his life to us, and I will never forget him.

❐   ❑   ❐

Mike Clark's tenure with Discovery Toys was longer but ended no less tragically.

In 1989, Mike found a mole on his scalp. It was a malignant melanoma and already so big that it had to be removed by a plastic surgeon. As a young man, Mike had worked as a summer lifeguard for many years under the hot California sun without sunscreen or a hat, which might have contributed to the disease. His doctors believed that they had caught the cancer in time, and I refused to think about it again.

Three years later he felt a much larger lump in the back of his neck. The first doctor he went to at that juncture thought it was a sinus infection. I remember saying, "I don't think you have any sinus nodes in the back of your neck," and I sent him to my ear, nose, and throat specialist for a second opinion. Sure enough, the cancer had returned. Mike underwent surgery at Stanford University Hospital a few weeks later to remove both the new tumor and a number of lymph nodes in his neck. Once again, his doctors were optimistic that they had caught the disease. Six weeks later another lump appeared, and after that it was mostly a matter of time.

Mike worked as long as he could, but after a few months he had to stay home. I often ignored the business in favor of spending as many hours with him as I could. Mike was alternately brave and heartbroken about leaving his three young sons and wife behind.

I often went to his house on short notice, since he couldn't predict when he would feel well enough to receive company. More than once I forgot a meeting at the office when I went running over to see him. Discovery Toys was doing close to $100 million in sales by that time, and we had approximately thirty thousand ECs. The business was able to do without me—but I would have been there for Mike anyway.

One day in December 1992, when Rich Newton, vice president of operations, and I were visiting him, Mike gave me his keys to the office and his company credit cards. It should have been clear to me that he was saying good-bye, but I didn't want to face it. In fact, I went back to work that afternoon telling myself that he was getting better because he had gripped my hand firmly and spoken with more strength than I had seen in weeks.

He passed away the next day at the age of forty-five. Grief is black, painful, and crazy-making. I remember little about the following year except that people assumed I had grieved when he was sick and should have been over it by then. ***No matter how sick a person becomes, the grieving process doesn't really start until the person has died.***

Over time, I discovered that you can learn to live without a loved one, but you never forget. I have often felt that Mike was sitting on my shoulder and continuing to share his wisdom with me. I am continually grateful that I had the ability to spend as much time with him during those final months as he would allow—and that I did not have to worry about being fired for doing it.

38. The Biggest Win

I HAVE YET ONE MORE personal story to share—which I hope will keep someone from making the same mistakes I have.

I am proud to say that I have been married to the same wonderful man for thirty-one years. When you have that kind of history with someone, when you can say that you not only deeply love but admire this person, when you still look forward to seeing him at the end of the day, then you know what it is to have a soul mate. You are the beneficiary of one of God's greatest gifts.

But Ed and I didn't simply say "I do" and buy a one-way ticket into the land of marital bliss. We married young and faced many of the challenges which come with that decision; we moved across country, supported each other through graduate school, and for a while were poor enough to qualify for food stamps.

And those were the easy years.

With Tara's birth, we had to realign the structure of our family, just as every couple must when they become parents. Then, when Tara was two, I launched Discovery Toys. You might say I now had two children: Tara was the first, the business the second. In any case, I worked so hard at both that I had little left over for my marriage.

Because Tara was so important to me, I chose to work only part time until she started first grade. After that, I gave her three hours of absolutely undivided attention every evening. Without fail, Ed would then take over for an hour or so. How much life together as a couple could we have after that?

Pacifica Imports, the manufacturing business that originally brought Ed and me to California, was grounded on a solid idea but had a gluttonous need for cash. Finally it went into bankruptcy.

Ed grieved for the loss of his business, a process I did not really allow myself to understand at the time. If there was any gift in Mike's and Jim's deaths for me, it was the empathy I have learned for others in grief. Today I would react quite differently to Ed's loss.

Although I was working my tail off, I was still going on the assumption that Ed was the breadwinner, not I. The idea that the family might look to my income scared me. I guess I really did not want that level of responsibility. In those early days, although I took my company very seriously, it still had aspects of being a fun game, not something that might eventually become number seventeen in *Inc.* magazine's list of the fastest-growing five hundred companies. Perhaps I was still mired in the prefeminist messages which dictated that I should be the stay-at-home wife while Ed put on his suit and tie and took the morning train to town—not that my behavior ever matched those messages! ***Look at your behavior to learn what you really think rather than what you say you think.***

A year later, Ed got a job teaching electronics, but after another year, he came home one day and told me that he had quit. I exploded: "What do you mean, you quit?"

Ed was genuinely surprised at my anger. He was frustrated with unmotivated students who were just putting in their time to get a degree. "I wouldn't expect you to do anything that you didn't want to do," he countered.

He was right. He would have supported me totally if I had left something I hated. I was running Discovery Toys because I loved it. I now realize that I hadn't appreciated his need to have a job that he loved, too.

We began to withdraw from one another. We often tried to talk but simply got nowhere. We were like boxers coming out of our corners when the bell rang, circling each other, throwing a cautious punch or two, never getting close enough to connect, and then retreating when the bell rang again, having accomplished nothing but to feel even more wary of each other than before. ***When you stop talking about the issues at hand, the real trouble begins.***

In retrospect, we should have gone to see a marriage counselor immediately. Counseling may be scary at first and even painful at times, but it's certainly easier and less painful than a divorce. I hope that at least one couple will learn from my near-disastrous mistake; I imagine there are many more who could.

Since we didn't see anybody, a couple of years went by, and things only worsened. After his stint in teaching, Ed became a market maker, like my brother-in-law, Walt. It was risky, stressful work that was completely unsuited to Ed's personality. Ed is a kind, nurturing person, while the culture of the stock market is often impersonal and ruthless. Any business whose entire mission is money does not spend any time worrying about developing its people.

On a practical level, too, his new profession separated us even further. The stock market opens at 6 A.M. Pacific time, so Ed was up by 4:30 every day. He was often asleep on his feet by the time I was ready for bed.

Finally, although Ed was quite successful in his own right, I was the one who was starting to get some attention from the media. I had been interviewed by *People* magazine and had appeared on several national morning television shows and *The Merv Griffin Show.* When

Ed accompanied me on my travels, it was always on our annual incentive trips and our conventions where we were surrounded by hundreds of happy couples and individuals who were thrilled to meet with us. We would travel first class, ride in limousines, and stay in the presidential suites that were given to us free by the hotel.

To Ed, it looked as though I were ruling the world with a giant rattle as scepter. Yet we were far from living like royalty at home. And he was never along for those business trips during the rest of the year when I stayed in cheap hotels, shared my room with a staff member, took buses to the airport, and stopped three times on the way to our destination because the airfare was less expensive.

Our disparate views of the company led to some painful power struggles over money. Why couldn't I bring more money home? If the company was so rich and we traveled so well, why couldn't he have all the toys he wanted? He felt like I was deliberately not sharing, and the insecurity and poverty of his refugee background came to the fore.

I, on the other hand, was putting every possible penny back into the company. There is a big difference between being paper-wealthy and having actual liquidity. I dealt with the harsh day-to-day realities of struggling to make enough profit so that the field would always be protected and the business would never again be vulnerable to banks or venture capitalists. I was working so hard that I really didn't care about having more money at home. I had no time to spend it anyway.

I was also struggling internally just as hard as he was; I had no role models for my part in all this. Was I too domineering, too masculine, not sexy enough? Physically, I take after my father more than my mother—no cause for shame. But that fact combined with my father having been a major role model and the knowledge that I was doing something with my working life that generally only men did made me wonder sometimes if was I going to wake up one morning and suddenly have become a man. I am truly grateful that society has evolved enough that my daughter can model herself on me as well as on Ed and avoid this particular struggle.

I had at least one thing in common with many women who have faced marital difficulties: I concluded that all the tensions in our marriage must be my fault, because if I were a better wife, all would be bliss. *In any complicated family situation, more than one person is responsible.*

❐   ❑   ❐

Out of the blue, one day in 1986, I woke up and my ambivalence was gone. It was OK to work and to be a mom; I was a great mom. It was OK to succeed; I was helping thousands of women and tens of thousands of families. I didn't have to feel guilty about my drive. I was OK—and I wanted a divorce.

Ed was out of town, finally taking a long-planned trip to Hungary, his childhood home. It was his first return since his hurried departure during the revolution of 1956 when his family smuggled him out in a mail sack. His rare absence had probably cleared the way for my revelation. It was not an entirely liberating thought, however. I felt as though I were living in a dark tunnel with no end and no light. No matter in which direction I turned, there was only pain for everyone. I started to waver. Maybe I really was the one causing it all. And yet, I had reached a point where I believed I couldn't stay with Ed.

My attorney, Roger Mertz, arranged for another attorney, Merrill Steinberg, who specialized in high-profile divorces, to consult with me. We met in Roger's San Francisco office, because he hoped I might feel more comfortable in familiar surroundings in a spacious conference room on the fortieth floor of one of the Embarcadero Towers in San Francisco's financial district.

Merrill Steinberg, the divorce lawyer, was a dark-browed, square-jawed man in his late forties, trim and respectable in a charcoal suit.

He took a very interesting tack. First he asked a lot of questions about my marriage. Then he painted a bleak and truthful picture of the process I was undertaking. I had built up Discovery Toys while married to Ed, so Ed owned half of it. If Ed and I divorced, I would probably have to sell the business in order to pay him his share of our community property. I might even have to pay alimony. Merrill warned me about the possibility of a custody battle and how, given our unique circumstances, Ed might even win.

Then Merrill asked me if Ed had ever been unfaithful, if he'd ever abused me. Indignantly, I replied "Never" to both questions. But he went on, almost as if my answers had been yes, proclaiming how hard we would fight to keep my assets from this lazy, predatory man and how hard we would fight to stop him from getting custody of his own child.

His attacks on my husband surprised and galvanized me. I found myself defending Ed. He was brilliant and hardworking, a patient and caring father.

At this, Merrill Steinberg smiled and said, "Mrs. Nemeth, I don't think you want a divorce. You love your husband—you're just not communicating with him. You don't need an attorney, believe me. I could make a great deal of money on this divorce, but what you really need is a marriage counselor. I know someone very good whom I'm going to call right now." ***Be open to the unexpected help that someone might give you.*** His words resonated, and I felt enormous relief. I knew in my heart that I still loved Ed. I hoped that counseling would help us open up to one another again. By the time I had returned to my office, forty-five minutes later, Merrill had already set up an appointment for me.

I was very lucky to encounter such a highly ethical man. Had he simply encouraged me in my original plans, given my vulnerable state, my life might have taken a much unhappier path.

A few days later, Ed returned from Hungary. When he stepped off the jetway, I saw a different man. His back was straighter, his head was held high, and he was just as handsome as he had been when I almost dropped spaghetti on him at camp twenty-one years ago.

On the way back from the airport, Ed talked nonstop about his trip. Returning, he had reconciled his past and present and had finally banished some of the demons that had pursued him all these years. He no longer felt as though half of him were floating somewhere in the unknown. I was excited for him. Having lived a pretty sheltered childhood, I hadn't realized that it had been quite so difficult for him all these years. *Sometimes when we're caught up in our troubles, we forget that others are dealing with their own issues as well.*

It was time to broach the subject. "I've been to see a marriage counselor," I said. "Will you go to see him with me, too?"

"Yes," he said softly, "I certainly will."

◻   ◻   ◻

Sometimes I hear women with troubled marriages complain, "He won't go with me to counseling, so what's the point?" Don't use that as an excuse. If he really won't go, then go on your own; perhaps he'll join you later. *Don't let others make decisions for you.* You can have enormous influence on another person if you have the skills and the desire. Counseling can help you figure out what your real desire is and give you the support you desperately need. You can also learn some specific skills that may help change the dynamics of your relationship or at least help you convince your husband to join you.

Ed and I laid out our conflicts. The counselor, a well-known psychologist, grasped the central issue immediately. He said, "Here's the deal, Lane. By California law, Ed owns half of Discovery Toys, so whether you like it or not, he's your partner. Start treating him that way.

And Ed, although you own 50 percent, it's Lane's company, and she ultimately controls the day-to-day decisions."

With that statement, the counselor pulled the plug on our power struggle. Like many couples, we had needed an outside perspective. But his statement was not a magic wand—there is no such thing.

We spent another six months in counseling. We learned how we had fallen into a vicious circle. The more I pulled away from Ed, the less he supported me, and the further I distanced myself. Thanks to the intervention of this gifted psychologist, we got the circle spinning the other way. Once again, we slowly learned to rebuild our trust in one another and to talk freely.

Now, every morning I wake up and thank God I didn't let this intelligent, nurturing, humorous man get away.

But I didn't tell him until many years later that I had been to see the lawyer before I went to see the counselor.

❐   ❑   ❐

Sometimes there's nothing you can do to save a marriage. Then it's better for the children, in the long run, if the parents make the split. Ed and I were so united in our determination that Tara not suffer that we had made a contingency plan: If things fell apart totally, we would let her stay in the house, and we would take turns living with her so she wouldn't have to move around. I knew in my heart that no matter how hard we tried, a divorce would yank the firm foundation we had so carefully built from beneath Tara's feet. She would have suffered even worse than the two of us and would also have needed counseling for a long time.

Thanks to an ethical lawyer and to a superb marriage counselor, none of this ever happened. And here's where I sincerely hope that my story will be of use. I find it interesting that most homeowners, upon discovering cracks in the foundation of their house, will see to the repairs immediately. Why would we give a marriage any less attention? Left untended, those cracks will only multiply until the house collapses.

Even today, with psychologists clogging the radio airwaves and television talk shows, couples too often see counseling as a sign of failure, a sign that they can't cope on their own. Where is it written that we are supposed to cope entirely on our own? We don't drill our own teeth, take out our own tonsils, or represent ourselves in court. Most of us don't even fix our own cars. We live in a complicated and interdependent society, and we face choices and challenges that our grandparents could never have imagined. In Ed's and my case, the opportunities I had created for myself were exciting but had left both of us without a map. The counseling helped us to create that map. *The world is changing so fast that maps of your life made yesterday may already be obsolete. The only constant we have in life is constant change. Accept help from others who may be more skilled at cartography than you are.*

❐   ❑   ❐

When Tara was two and completely unable to do simple one-piece puzzles, and when, as she grew, she could not play any other spatially-oriented game, I knew she had a learning disability. I "officially" discovered this when she was in fifth grade and underwent extensive testing with an educational psychologist. She was very bright and had a phenomenal memory, but certain abstract concepts were initially difficult for her to grasp. In fact, it was in trying to teach her arithmetic that I had the inspiration for Measure Up!® cups. Learning-disabled kids—and there are many, all too often undiagnosed—can usually benefit from any tool that makes the abstract more concrete and helps them learn a subject using a variety of learning styles. The Measure Up!® cups, for example, use three learning styles. Tara was a kinesthetic learner while she poured, an auditory learner as I repeated for her that one and one adds up to two, and a visual learner as she poured the sand from one cup to another. We used colored sand to make it more visible. Another example is that I helped her learn the alphabet by having her trace each letter in the sand, feeling each letter written in large pieces of sandpaper, and drawing each letter on her back with a finger.

Thanks to the success of Discovery Toys, when Tara was in high school, Ed had the freedom to stay home and tutor her. By this time, math and science were way above my abilities. In fact, some areas of science had progressed so far since Ed had been to school that occasionally he'd have to spend the mornings studying himself so that in the afternoon he could tutor Tara on the subject. He was a natural teacher, patient and loving, and he had a student who cared.

Ed's staying home was a role reversal. It was not an easy role to play, but it was right for our family. I believe that if society would allow couples to truly follow their hearts, many more men would happily be home with the children while their wives were happily working.

Tara graduated magna cum laude from Brandeis University and is heading for a Ph.D. in child psychology. Without Ed's devotion to Tara in high school, the time I spent with her as needed, her own intrinsic motivation, Discovery Toys products, and many wonderful teachers along the way, she would never be where she is today.

But I feel that's only part of the story. The three of us are now bonded together in a way that brings to mind a rather corny sampler I once saw in a giftshop. It read, "A Happy Family Is an Early Heaven." But as you have seen, it wasn't always so blissful. *Even in matters of the heart, success takes persistence.*

39. The Quest

FROM THE FIRST YEARS of Discovery Toys, I yearned for a way to break out of the seasonality of the toy business. The vast majority of toys—60 to 70 percent—are bought in anticipation of the holidays. This can make for some lean months in the middle of the year.

My desire to expand also emerged from my vision of Discovery Toys not really as a toy company but rather as a parenting company. This was why we held workshops and demos, why we brought women together to share their experiences, why it was so important to us to provide alternatives to working moms.

It was this vision that led to my idea for Body Pals®, which we launched in 1994. My thinking was that parents and children already didn't have enough time together, so why should they spend any of it locked into battles over taking baths or washing hair? Together with a laboratory we developed a line of soaps, shampoos and that rinsed out in one rinse, bubble baths, a de-tangler that got out the worst tangles easily yet left no film on the hair, and water-soluble body paints that were actually soap.

The products were beautifully illustrated and packaged to appeal to the preschooler. After their introduction, we realized that the six-to-

ten-year-old market—kids too old to respond to most cartoon charac-
ters but still too young to think of shampoo as a way to get dates—was
a seriously neglected group. We repackaged and in some cases reformu-
lated the line to suit their growing needs, too.

Sadly, the line was never really successful. We used premium
ingredients, so we were never able to get the price down low enough to
compete with the average shampoo on the supermarket shelf. Also,
when we introduced the products, we didn't have the infrastructure in
place for a customer convenience ship program so that the customer
could get a new bottle each month automatically.

Nevertheless, because I believed that people would come to see
that it was worth spending an extra dollar on an exceptional product,
we kept Body Pals® until a few years ago, when we finally decided that
they weren't pulling their weight in expensive catalog space.

**No matter what you believe or wish for, your customer
always makes the final decision.**

❐   ❑   ❐

Several years after launching Body Pals®, we tried clothes. Once again,
my vision of the product was motivated by my desire to help parents
and children.

Toddlers and preschoolers go through an important developmental period in which they struggle to become more independent. They
want to dress themselves and to choose their own clothes. This can
cause problems for parents who, no matter how much they support
their children, still feel embarrassed to be seen with a kid wearing a
fuchsia plaid shirt and green-striped shorts, with at least one of those
items on backwards.

We designed our clothes so that each piece went with every other
piece, no matter what top or bottom or jacket or socks you put on.
There were no buttons or zippers, and some were even made so that

you could wear them backwards, forwards, or inside out. A kid just learning to dress himself could earn a sense of achievement, and mom or dad could smile because he always looked stylish. The clothes were also so phenomenally comfortable that kids wanted to sleep in them.

The first year we sold $5 million worth of these clothes. What could go wrong?

Everything. First of all, the margins in the clothing industry are even tighter than in the toy industry, and we were already working pretty close to the edge. On top of the cost of making our clothes comfortable and long-wearing, our distribution channels have a number of levels and each level adds to the cost, so it was hard for us to make our prices appealing. The prices we paid the model makers, cutters, designers, and manufacturers were already unusually high due to the high quality of the clothes.

We make many of our toys offshore, and we know how to find factories that comply with our strict guidelines for working conditions. But when we launched the clothing line, we were too small to go offshore, so we decided to manufacture in the United States. Imagine my profound horror when I visited these vendors and discovered that the conditions under which some Americans were working were ten times worse than anything I had ever seen overseas. I was not about to be involved in a process that would so horrendously exploit workers; this was hardly why I started my company.

Yet another problem was that our field had trouble with the change. Many of our ECs feared they were spreading themselves too thin. How would they run their demos—thirty minutes on toys and twenty on clothes? Were we compromising our vision? Our field feared that this might be the case.

Don't stray from your mission.

Finally, our toys and games were picked from a completely automated line, with an error rate of about .05 percent. The clothes, on the other hand, arrived with sizes, colors, and patterns all mixed together. We were unable to put them on the automated picker, so we had to hire a lot of additional help to ship them to our customers—not a cost-effective move.

Although after a year we made a decision to get out of the clothing game, I actually count it as a success. The world is a different place at the turn of the millennium than it was in the 1970s. Any business that does not continue to try new ideas and react quickly to an ever-changing environment will not succeed.

We must learn to value change, not to fear it.

❐   ❑   ❐

Despite our need to try new ventures, had Mike Clark still been with me, I'm convinced we never would have branched out into clothing. He would have uncovered the traps we fell into ahead of time. It's the very least of all the reasons I miss him.

Mistakes don't stop with passing years—not if you're taking risks.

These false starts did lead me to what has been a very successful expansion: Discovery Quest, our line of books and educational software.

Beginning in the mid-'90s, we started offering high-quality educational software for sale. All the programs we carry have been carefully screened, and many are exclusively ours. Our software is guaranteed 100 percent violence-free—I would say there's enough shooting, killing, and blowing things up in the real world that we don't need to simulate it. Violent software is much more dangerous than violent television or movies, and we all know how bad those are for our children! Movies and television are passive experiences. Interactive software means that you become the person killing or maiming another. Our brains have a very hard time distinguishing "play" from reality in an interactive situation such as this. We called our software line Discovery Quest. When we added books for individual sale in 1998, we made Discovery Quest a separate part of our catalog.

Unlike toys, books and software are bought all year round. It's helped us level out our seasonality. This division has been a real success, but as with so many successes, it required people who were able to learn from failures.

40. How to Turn Your Child into a Lifelong Reader

READING WITH YOUR CHILD is one of the most important things you can do for him. You stimulate his imagination by encouraging him to form pictures in his mind; you develop his logical processes as he follows a story; you help him expand his attention span; and you develop a child who will be motivated to read on his own.

It's critically important to continue to read aloud to your child after he has learned to read. A second-grader's reading vocabulary may be only several hundred words, but his auditory vocabulary and his ability to comprehend a story may be several grade levels above that. Reading aloud to him more complex stories than he is able to read to himself fosters his imagination, attention span, and vocabulary.

Reading aloud also allows you to share a special time with your child. In fact, I advise parents that when they are locked in a power struggle with their child or feel their temper about to explode, whip out a book. Sit down and read. Suddenly you're touching—and nothing counteracts anger like a gentle touch. At the same time you're entering an entirely different, magical world of the imagination—together. The anger will quickly be forgotten.

Combine learning and closeness.

We all want our children to read for a lifetime. But that won't happen by itself. Whatever improvements we might all want to see in education, we as parents cannot pass that particular buck onto the schools.

Here's how to give your child one of the most precious gifts of all, the gift of the love of books:

Books aren't just for bedtime anymore. Read to your child at every opportunity. A few minutes at bedtime won't cut it—it's a lovely ritual, but not enough. Your child, and most likely you, are too tired to maximize the benefit. Make reading a daylong activity—after lunch, before naptime, as a substitute for television. I've already pointed out how you can use a book as an almost magic anger-defusing device.

Whenever or for whatever reason you and your child are reading together, don't limit your role to just reading the words aloud. Ask age-appropriate questions: "What do you think is coming next? What would you do if you were a dog and you thought nobody wanted to take you home? How do you think the elephant feels now that he's living in the zoo?"

Take your children to the library. Get your child a library card and make a weekly trip to your local branch. If necessary, you and the children's librarian can help your child make her selections. The following week, return those books and take out new ones. Your child learns responsibility and looks forward to the routine of this activity she shares with you. Not only does she get to experience new books, but you do as well. After a while, I simply could not pick up the same book for what seemed like the millionth time. The library was a lifesaver for me.

Treat books as precious items. Each of our Discovery Toys books arrives with a bookplate because we want to reinforce the idea that books are items to cherish and to be proud of. There are many lovely bookplates available at your local bookstore as well.

Give your child a bookshelf of his own, or at least a special shelf in the family bookcase. Let her see that books are not for doorstops or booster seats. When your family has outgrown a series of books, donate any books that are in decent condition to your favorite charity, such as a shelter for the homeless, a shelter for abused women and children, the local library, or your school. Take your child with you and let her make the presentation.

Let your children see you read. Your child looks to you as a role model in all areas. It will not be easy to turn your children into readers if they never see you pick up a book. When your child sees you buy or borrow books, care for them, and most of all, read them, he will naturally imitate you. Reading worthy periodicals or newspapers makes for good role modeling, too. There's a big world out there, and you will want your child to keep up with it when he's ready.

Encourage your children to make their own books. There are many ways to make books. Kids can write on loose-leaf paper, or they can dictate to you while you type. You can have it bound at a photocopy shop for a few dollars or bind it yourself with yarn and construction paper. The right computer software will let you include pictures, but the low-tech solution is every bit as good if not better: let your child cut pictures from magazines or draw his own to illustrate his book.

Practice experiential reading with your child. If your child draws a picture, have him tell you about it, and write down his words on the picture or on the back of it. Then read back to him what you've written, pointing out his words. Eventually he will connect those black squiggles with words.

Read out loud to your child as long as he or she will allow you to.
Children's hearing vocabulary, and their comprehension, is many grade
levels above their reading vocabulary. A second-grader who is able to
read only simple books with a few sentences per page may adore hearing E. B. White's wonderful *Charlotte's Web*. Reading continues for
many years to be a lovely bedtime ritual as well as a way to calm everyone down during the day.

❐   ❑   ❐

Just as children go through developmental stages such as sitting, crawl-
ing, standing, and walking, they also go through stages of literacy
development. These stages of learning literacy are on a continuum.
Each stage overlaps and moves into the next. In these stages, children
need to experience language in all its forms: written, read, sung, and
spoken.

"The Stages of Literacy Development" on pages 248–252 lists
typical behaviors of literacy development in children of different age
groups, ways parents can help, and appropriate books for each age
group. You can help engage your child in reading at each stage.

The Discovery Toys "Reading Together at Home" program, developed in conjunction with the Primary Center for Language Development in England, is full of books and activities that will go a long way
toward encouraging a reader.

As your child grows, she'll want to choose more and more books
for herself; even comic books are fine. The important point is that your
child is reading at all. And don't forget to keep reading yourself—before
you know it, she'll be reading Tolstoy and you'll want to be able to
keep up!

THE STAGES OF LITERACY DEVELOPMENT

INFANTS

BEHAVIOR:

❑ They look at, chew, pound on, and toss books.

❑ They bat at or put a finger on pictures in a book and eventually ask, "What's that?"

❑ They babble and look for responses to their attempts at speaking.

PARENTS' ROLES:

❑ Give infants books that can tolerate their exploration.

❑ By responding, speaking, singing, and reading to them, parents help to build a bond, develop language, and validate a baby's attempts at interacting.

APPROPRIATE BOOKS:

❑ Vinyl, cloth, and cardboard books.

❑ Books that have very simple, clear, and bright illustrations.

TODDLERS

BEHAVIOR:

❑ They continually ask questions as they explore their world.

❑ They may have favorite stories they want to hear over and over.

❑ They scribble and draw as early forms of writing.

❑ Toddlers need lots of verbal interaction and support of their curiosity through having their questions answered.

❑ Sing songs and say rhymes with your child.

❑ Toddlers should be allowed to choose their favorite books and hear them many times.

❑ Providing paper and markers or crayons to toddlers facilitates their learning. Being nonjudgmental of the "writing" toddlers produce gives them the message that they are capable.

APPROPRIATE BOOKS:

❑ Stories with predictable plots.

❑ Very simple storybooks about everyday things that are familiar to the toddler.

❑ Favorite books.

❑ Books that can be sung.

❑ Rhyming books.

❑ Books with prominent illustrations that are full of information and match the text.

PRESCHOOLERS

BEHAVIOR:

Many of the behaviors of the previous age group, plus

❑ They love to "read" to parents, stuffed toys, and themselves.

❑ They are increasingly able to memorize, retell, and act out stories.

❑ Parents should continue to support literacy behavior from the previous age group and make reading to preschoolers a regular part of the day.

❑ Listen attentively when preschoolers "read" and don't worry about inaccuracies. For preschoolers, mimicking reading is an important literacy behavior and is just as valuable as a child's first step.

❑ Be supportive of all writing attempts they make.

APPROPRIATE BOOKS:

Everything from the previous age group, plus

❑ Storybooks that can be easily acted out.

❑ Books with rich, descriptive language.

❑ Simple factual books and books that pose questions.

PRIMARY-SCHOOL STUDENTS (GRADES K–3)

BEHAVIOR:

Many of the behaviors of the previous age group, plus

❑ They enjoy hearing and reading a variety of books that are above and below their reading level.

❑ They love to play with words and tell jokes and riddles.

❑ They are becoming more and more proficient as readers.

❑ They are becoming more and more proficient as writers.

Everything from the previous age group, plus

❑ Read—to your child and with your child—a variety of books at varying levels of sophistication and length.

❑ Language play helps children think about sounds, words, and meaning. Join in the silliness! Play letter, sound, and word guessing games.

❑ Encourage children's interest in books and their developing reading skills—but expect some errors in reading.

❑ Give children plenty of opportunity to express themselves in writing and drawing. Don't be critical—as children grow and develop, skills and grammar become more and more developed and incorporated into their writing.

APPROPRIATE BOOKS:

Everything from the previous age group, plus

❑ Simple reference books.

❑ Books that are easy, as well as challenging, to read alone and with an adult.

❑ Books that include a topic which is of special interest to the child.

❑ Simple riddle books.

❑ First readers and beginning chapter books.

❑ Blank journals.

ELEMENTARY-SCHOOL STUDENTS (GRADES 3–6)

BEHAVIOR:

All of the behaviors of the previous age group, plus

❏ The children are becoming much more skilled and proficient as readers.

❏ They are becoming more proficient and skilled as writers.

PARENTS' ROLES:

Everything from the previous age group, plus

❏ Show interest in what your children want to read.

❏ Discuss books as well as authors with them.

❏ Offer them the opportunity to write for a variety of purposes and audiences.

❏ Play word games and do crossword puzzles.

APPROPRIATE BOOKS:

Everything from the previous age group, plus

❏ Reference books.

❏ Books that are of varied writing styles.

❏ Longer chapter books.

❏ Books that are written by a variety of authors.

41. New Beginnings

COMPARED TO OUR EARLY YEARS, the later years at Discovery Toys were calm. Granted, that may be like saying that tropical storms don't drop as much water as typhoons—but we weathered what came our way.

With the passing of Jim and then Mike, things changed for me. And in 1997, I turned fifty; I think one often looks at the world somewhat differently after that milestone.

The business had grown to an unrecognizable size. By the early '90s, we had over thirty thousand ECs and were doing close to $100 million in business. We'd traveled a great distance since the days when UPS was bringing Richard Bendett's toys straight to my apartment door and a couple of schoolteachers were turning around to sell them.

But those flying-by-the-seat-of-your-pants beginnings are what an entrepreneur thrives on, and I missed them. My greatest capabilities lie in launching projects, in generating ideas and taking chances. I never saw myself as a high-level manager, and here I was at the helm of a rather large corporation. *Stay true to your strengths.*

Over the years I had been approached by a number of companies much larger than we who were interested in buying us. I had always said no. In fact, once when my late but not lamented venture capitalist had pressed me to take the company public, I replied, "Selling Discovery Toys would be like selling my second child." (His response, "Only a woman would say that," made me wonder how far women had actually come in society—or how far some men had come in their thinking, for that matter.)

But in the late '90s, I was ready for a change. After all, Tara had grown up and left for college. Maybe Discovery Toys could go on while I played a different role in it.

Once the word was out that I was willing to sell, interested buyers began quickly to appear. I, however, had a personal first choice of my own: Avon Products, Inc.

I always had a great deal of respect for Avon. Unlike some other direct-sales companies, there was never a hint of scandal about them. Their ethics and culture were similar to ours, and they had been in business for well over a hundred years. I knew they could offer us not only huge additional resources but invaluable experience.

The CEO and chairman of Avon was Jim Preston, a man whom I had liked and admired since meeting him through the Direct Selling Association many years before. I knew that he would treat any of my inquiries with respect. However, I decided to approach him a bit obliquely.

I wrote to Jim asking if he were interested doing a joint venture with us in China—a country whose people, I am convinced, will take Discovery Toys to its heart someday. His response was, "Your idea is not appealing to us at this time, but if you're interested in selling to Avon, I'm interested in talking."

This, of course, was what I wanted all along; I was hoping that Jim would bring up the subject. ***When another party approaches you with an idea or request, you are in a better negotiating position than if you were to approach that person.***

A few days later I flew to New York, and Jim and I had what I will always consider a historic dinner at the Oak Room at the Plaza Hotel. Our conversation confirmed for me that Jim was in tune with the mission of Discovery Toys. By the time the check for our dinner arrived, we had shaken hands on our mutual desire to do a deal. The details we left to the attorneys and accountants.

❐   ❑   ❐

One of my big concerns about the sale of the company—and one of the reasons I had waited so long to do it—was that I was concerned about what would happen to the thousands of women who sell our toys. My responsibility to them had informed many of my decisions over the years, and this one was no different.

As soon as the details of the sale had been finalized, I immediately started planning a series of workshops across the country where I could meet with all our ECs, explain the transition, and hopefully, allay any fears they might have. And of course they did have fears. Were they going to lose their Discovery Toys identity? Was the mission of our company altered? Was I going to disappear?

I did not disappear; in fact, I was able to be more present. For years I had borne the stress of running the company more or less alone, and I was beginning to feel like the statue of Atlas at Rockefeller Center who holds up the world. As big as we had become from one perspective, we were still often one small mistake away from disaster. Now I had a multibillion-dollar corporation behind me. Where once we had been resource-poor, now we were resource-rich.

I spent the next six months doing tens of thousands of miles of traveling, getting reacquainted with our field, and looking at ways to refresh the entire company. We hired six regional managers to work with our ECs, helping them write business plans and redefine success for themselves.

Getting back in the field also reenergized me! I began to think more creatively than I had since Mike's death, and I was planning new product once again. Our 1998 line was the best we had had in several years: Tactominoes®, Baby's Photo Cube®, and Hammer Away!® were some of our big hits—not to mention the long-awaited and now award-winning Picture Perfect Melody Mobile™.

1998 was also the year we introduced "Reading Together at Home," a series of books and activities designed to help parents help their children learn to love to read.

I was in Nuremberg at the toy show the day we finalized the sale; I had already signed the papers, but the lawyers had to call to verify that I was alive the day the transfer took place. I expected to go through a period of grief, but I never did—the changes were too positive. **When the time is right, big changes can feel good.**

Unbelievably, only eighteen months later my life was about to change again. Jim Preston was retiring, and the new CEO felt that Discovery Toys did not fit into their strategic plan. The prospect of selling the company a second time in less than two years sent me temporarily into shock. Then I got busy.

Once again my phone was ringing off the hook, but this time the process was much more difficult; I didn't have a buyer in mind or the desire to find one. Nevertheless, in partnership with Avon, I needed to find a company who would love and cherish Discovery Toys. I met with a number of prospective buyers, but none interested me. Then I was fortunate enough to receive a call from Tony Callandra, president of McGuggan, a small group of private investors who had initially contacted me during my negotiations with Avon. Over the next six months we all got to know each other very well, and my management team and I were convinced it would be a happy marriage. **People with the same goals find each other.**

Avon still believes in us, and they decided to retain a small interest in the business. As for me, there were two very positive changes: First of all, I got back a piece of the ownership, and my role went from CEO to chairman.

What this means is that I'm still involved in the business, mostly overseeing the product and public relations, but I no longer oversee its daily operations—nor even go into work every day!

It's not that I want to retire. Entrepreneurs never retire—not as long as they can find someone to listen to their ideas! Rather, it's time for me to become a grandmother to my second child, Discovery Toys. I can hardly wait until my first child is ready to make me a grandmother as well, although it will be a number of years yet.

Of course, I have ideas for new businesses, but I also want to spend some time mentoring other entrepreneurs. Ever since Mike died, I have felt a need to share my years of experience with other young entrepreneurs. As I know only too well, entrepreneurs starting out usually can't afford to hire professional consultants. I hope to help others avoid some of my mistakes and benefit from what is now my more than twenty years of business experience.

❐   ❑   ❐

Another area I plan to direct my energy into is the well-being of our nation's children. Infant day care is one of the fastest-growing segments of the day-care industry. But the ratio of adults to babies remains unacceptable, as does the ratio of adults to three- and four-year-olds as well. Although those adults are taking care of our most precious children for eight to nine hours a day, they are usually neither trained nor paid adequately.

Too often, mothers don't have enough choice about who is going to care for their children. For the cost of a few Stealth bombers, we could provide substantial subsidies to day-care centers for use in improving the training and pay of all childcare workers. This alone would help improve care by making those jobs more desirable and decreasing the turnover.

We need to see longer maternity leaves for mothers and paternity leaves for dads—fully paid for at least one parent, both of which are standard in some other countries. I'd also like to see parenting classes widely available at low cost or even free—at a convenient time, and with childcare available. How about a nonprofit National Parenting Center that oversees these classes, ensuring that they meet certain standards? Maybe a National Parenting Association will be my next business.

In short, I want what I've wanted all along: to see every child have the opportunity to reach his or her maximum potential with the help of the best parenting and the best educational tools there are.

❐ ❑ ❐

New endings, new beginnings. I look forward to many more projects. Perhaps some will be even more exciting and challenging than Discovery Toys. But it will always be my second child.

I hope that some mistakes I've made, some lessons I've learned, perhaps some anecdote I've shared, will be of use. Life is full of Learning Moments, and I'm a perpetual student. I hope that from my story of growing Discovery Toys you have learned something about growing your own dream—and discovering your own way.

THE PRINCIPLES OF WISE PARENTING

ATTENTION
In addition to providing food and shelter, your caring attention
is vital to your child's happiness, self-worth, and growth.

LOVE
Accept your child unconditionally without being judgmental.

PATIENCE
Be gentle and patient with your child and yourself.

MUTUAL RESPECT
As a guide and role model, respect your child's individuality—
keep in mind that you do not own your child.

PLAY
Communicate and connect with your child by
participating in play—your child's work.

ENCOURAGEMEMT
Help your child build self-motivation and self-love by encouraging your child's accomplishments—not what pleases you.

RESPONSIBILITY
Empowering your child to make choices and decisions will
allow responsibility to take root.

MISTAKES
Mistakes are essential ingredients for growth and learning—
so don't expect perfection from your child or yourself.

HOME
Make your home a haven of safety—a world in which everyone in the family can truly be themselves and be valued.

Acknowledgments

I WISH TO OFFER THANKS first to Linda Carter, who originally pushed me to write a book. To Donna Levin, who guided me every step of the way. To my publishers, Richard Cohn and Cindy Black of Beyond Words Publishing, Inc., who had continued faith in me, even when I missed the first deadline. To Rosemary Williams, Marvin Moore, and Kathy Matthews, who provided excellent editorial support. To my friend and partner, Claudia Parker, who has seen me through some really difficult times and never lost patience. And to Neal Kavanaugh, who helped me organize my thoughts in the first place.

Above all I need to acknowledge the phenomenally dedicated staff of Discovery Toys, who have spent long, selfless hours, months, and years ensuring that Discovery Toys was able to survive even in its darkest hours. And to our Educational Consultants, who care so much about our mission and opportunity. Because of their dedication, belief, love, and talent, hundreds of thousands of families have had the opportunity to give their children the best in developmental and educational play, now and in the future.

Resources

FACT: OWNERS OF FULL-TIME, home-based businesses have incomes that are 20 percent higher than the income of the average household, according to the New York research firm IDC/Link. They also report that almost 11 percent of households that include a home-based business had an income last year of more than $100,000.

RESOURCES FOR BUSINESSES

Service Corps of Retired Executives: www.score.org
> This nonprofit organization offers free counseling to small businesses by retired executives.

Quicken: www.quicken.com/smallbusiness
> Among other products, you can download business forms from this site.

BizMove: www.bizmove.com
> "A small-business knowledge base."

BizPlus: www.bizplus.com
> This site calls itself the Internet Small Business Center and has numerous links for small-business information.

Microsoft Smallbiz: www.microsoft.com/smallbiz

U.S. Small Business Administration: www.sba.gov; 1-800-827-5722
Like all government offices, this site can be a chore to maneuver
in, but it has information galore.

U.S. Chamber of Commerce: www.uschamber.org

Yahoo Business: www.yahoo.com/business
Use this search engine to find endless business sites of interest.

Forbes Digital Tool: www.forbes.com
Check out the "Starting Your Own Business" articles in the
Small-Business Center.

Federal Trade Commission: www.ftc.gov
See the Business Guidance section.

Inc.Online: www.inc.com
Inc. magazine.

RESOURCES FOR HOME-BASED BUSINESSES

The National Association of the Self-Employed: www.nase.org;
262-462-2100

The Home Office Association of America: 212-980-4622

American Home Business Association: www.homebusiness.com;
1-800-758-8500

Direct Selling Association: 1666 K Street, NW, Suite 1010,
Washington, D.C. 20006-2808; 202-293-5760; fax: 202-463-4569;
www.dsa.org

Discovery Toys: 1-800-426-4777; www.discoverytoysinc.com

Home Business Made Easy: How to Select and Start a Home Business That Fits Your Interests, Lifestyle, and Pocketbook. David Hanania. Grants Pass, Ore.: Oasis Press, 1992.

The Home Office and Small Business Answer Book: Solutions to the Most Frequently Asked Questions about Starting and Running Home Offices and Small Businesses. Janet Attard. New York: Henry Holt, 1993.

How to Run Your Own Home Business. Coralee Smith Kern and Tammara Hoffman Wolfgram. Lincolnwood, Ill.: NTC Publishing, Passport Books, 1989.

How to Start a Successful Home Business. Karen Cheney and Lesley Alderman. New York: Warner Books, 1997.

The Joy of Working from Home. Jeff Berner. San Francisco: Berrett-Koehler Publications, 1994.

Launching Your Home-Based Business. David Bangs Jr. and Andi Axman. Dover, N.H.: Upstart Publishing, 1997.

Marketing for the Home-Based Business. Jeffrey P. Davidson. Holbrook, Mass: Bob Adams, 1990.

RESOURCES FOR WOMEN IN BUSINESS

Digital Women: www.digital-women.com
   Provides tools for women to succeed in business.

IVillage—the Women's Network: www.ivillage.com

Women's Wire—Small Business Smarts: www.womenswire.com
   This site assists in the process of creating business plans for small businesses.

RESOURCES FOR NETWORKING
WITH OTHER WOMEN IN BUSINESS

Business Women's Network: 1-800-48-WOMEN; www.bwni.com

The Small Business Administration Office of Women's Business Ownership: www.sba.gov

The American Business Women's Association: www.abwahq.org

National Association of Women Business Owners: www.nawbo.org

Women Entrepreneurs Online Network: www.weon.com
Promotes mentorship and networking among members.

FINANCING HELP FOR WOMEN ENTRPRENEURS

U.S. Small Business Administration: www.sba.gov

Capital Quest: www.usbusiness.com

America's Business Funding Directory: www.businessfinance.com

Commercial Finance Associations: www.cfr.com

BANKS

Wells Fargo Bank has pledged $10 billion for lending to women in business.

Bank of America (Nations Bank), First Union Bank, and Bank Boston Bank are among many who are interested in supporting women.

NETWORKING/INFORMATION
IN YOUR AREA OF EXPERTISE

Trade Show Central: www.tscentral.com
Comprehensive list of trade shows, conferences, and seminars on everything from accounting to zoology.

SEARCH ENGINE SITES

www.About.com

www.AltaVista.com

www.askjeeves.com

www.excite.com

www.infoseek.com

www.lycos.com

www.yahoo.com

http://www.allonesearch.com

http://www.locate.com

http://www.toptenlinks.com

http://merlin.cflc.lib.fl.us

http://www.searchenginewatch.com

http://www.electricmonk.com

SHOPPING SITES

http://www.roboshopper.com

http://www.acses.com

http://www.bottomdollar.com/index.html

http://www.mysimon.com

COMPUTER HARDWARE

CompareNet: www.compare.net

http://www.uvision.com

http://www.pricescan.com

http://www.killerapp.com

http://www.shopper.com

CUSTOMIZABLE METASEARCH SOFTWARE

http://www.Inforian.com

http://www.copernic.com

E-MAIL PLUS

Magical Desk: www.magicaldesk.com
Six on-line applications: e-mail, calendar, to-do list, address
book, bookmarks, and file storage.

Eudora Light: www.eudora.com
Eudora itself is very complicated, but Eudora light is close to
Outlook Express.

Outlook Express: www.outlookexpress.com
A great Microsoft product.

OFFICE SUPPLIES

Office Max: www.officemax.com

IPrint: www.iPrint.com
Print your business cards, stationery, etc.

Staples: www.staples.com

Office Depot: www.officedepot.com

Bottom Dollar: www.bottomdollar.com
"The Shopping Search Engine" lets you search for office
products available on-line.

NetMarket: www.netmarket.com
NetMarket claims to offer 800,000 brand-name products at
discount prices.

BT Office Products International: www.btopi.com
Full-service distributor of office products, furniture, and supplies;
also offers ergonomic and socially responsible products.

Furniture ReSolutions International: www.tradein.com
Buy or sell used office furniture.

BizRate: www.bizrate.com

Type in the name of the on-line merchant you are considering
and BizRate will tell you how past customers rate the site.

BEST TELEPHONE RATES
http://abelltolls.com

BUSINESS TRAVEL

Business Tools Travel Section: www.netpad.com/tools/travel.html

Map Quest: www.mapquest.com

This site will create maps to guide you from door to door and
city to city.

Travelocity: www.travelocity.com

Through the Sabre system you can see schedules for more than
700 airlines, make reservations, and get tickets. You can also
make reservations for more than 400 hotels as well as car
rentals.

Biztravel: www.biztravel.com

This site factors in your preferences when you book a flight,
hotel, or rental car, creates an itinerary that earns you the most
frequent-flyer miles, and keeps track of the mileage in your
account.

AUCTIONS

www.lycos.com/auction
http://www.haggle.com
http://www.onsale.com
http://dealdeal.com
http://www.ebay.com

DIRECTORIES

Big Yellow: www.bigyellow.com

Excite Education: www.excite.com/education/reference/phone_and_
email_directories

World Pages: www.worldpages.com

BUSINESS BOOKS

Amazon.com: www.amazon.com

Barnes and Noble: www.bn.com

CHILDCARE RESOURCES

Child Care Aware: 1-800-424-2246

National Association of Child Care Resource and Referral Agencies:
202-393-5501; www.childcarerr.org

The International Nanny Association: 1-800-297-1477;
www.nanny.org

National Association for the Education of Young Children:
1-800-424-2460; www.naeyc.org

PARENTING

Caring for Your School-Age Child: Ages 5 to 12. Edward L. Schor, ed.
New York: Bantam Doubleday Dell, 1995.

The Challenges of Parenthood. Rudolf Dreikurs. New York:
NAL/Dutton, Plume Books, 1991.

Child Behavior: The Classic Childcare Manual from the Gesell Institute of Human Development. Frances L. Ilg and Louise B. Ames. New York: HarperCollins, HarperPerennial, 1992. (I found the best part of this book to be "Ages and Stages," which I referred to often when Tara's behavior made a major change.)

Discipline without Tears. Rudolf Dreikurs. New York: NAL/Dutton, Plume Books, 1991. (Both of Dreikurs's excellent books discuss his theory of Natural Consequences.)

Infants and Mothers: Differences in Development. T. Berry Brazelton. New York: Delacorte Press, 1983.

Logical Consequences: A New Approach to Discipline. Rudolf Dreikurs and Loren Grey. New York: NAL/Dutton, 1990.

The Magic Years: Understanding and Handling the Problems of Early Childhood. Selma H. Fraiberg. New York: Simon and Schuster, Fireside, 1996.

Touchpoints: Your Child's Emotional and Behavioral Development. T. Berry Brazelton. Redding, Mass: Addison-Wesley, 1992.

Your Baby and Child: From Birth to Age Five. Penelope Leach and Jenny Matthews. New York: Alfred A. Knopf, 1997.

Your Two-Year-Old: Terrible or Tender. Louise B. Ames, Frances L. Ilg, and Carol C. Haber. New York: Delacorte Press, 1993.

Your Four-Year-Old: Wild and Wonderful. Frances L. Ilg, Louise B. Ames, and Carol C. Haber. New York: Dell Publishing, 1989.

Your Six-Year-Old: Loving and Defiant. Louise B. Ames, Frances L. Ilg, and Carol C. Haber. New York: Dell Publishing, 1981.

COMMUNICATION WITH YOUR CHILDREN

Between Parent and Child: New Solutions to Old Problems. Haim G. Ginott. New York: Avon Books, 1976.

Between Parent and Teenager. Haim G. Ginott. New York: Avon Books, 1982.

How to Have Intelligent and Creative Conversations with Your Kids. Jane M. Healy. New York: Doubleday Books, 1994.

How to Talk So Kids Will Listen and Listen So Kids Will Talk. Adele Faber and Elaine Mazlish. New York: Avon Books, 1982.

Siblings without Rivalry: How to Help Your Children Live Together So You Can Live Too. Adele Faber and Elaine Mazlish. New York: Avon Books, 1988.

COGNITIVE DEVELOPMENT

Endangered Minds: Why Our Children Don't Think—and What We Can Do about It. Jane M. Healy. New York: Simon and Schuster, Touchstone Books, 1990.

Failure to Connect: How Computers Affect Our Children's Minds— for Better and Worse. Jane M. Healy. New York: Simon and Schuster, 1998.

Nurturing Spirituality in Children
Author: Peggy J. Jenkins, Ph.D.
$10.95, softcover
Children who develop a healthy balance of mind and spirit enter adulthood with high self-esteem, better able to respond to life's challenges. Many parents wish to heighten their children's spiritual awareness but have been unable to find good resources. *Nurturing Spirituality in Children* offers scores of simple lessons that parents can teach to their children in less than ten minutes at a time.

FOR CHILDREN

Girls Know Best: Advice for Girls from Girls on Just About Everything
Editor: Michelle Roehm
$8.95, softcover
Girls Know Best contains the writings of thirty-eight different girls from across the United States. The book is divided into chapters focusing on specific issues and giving advice from the girl writers to the girl readers. The topics include living with siblings, school/homework, parents, divorce and dealing with stepfamilies, boys, friends, losses when your best friend moves away or you do, depression, dealing with differences (race and religion), drugs, our bodies and looks, and overcoming life's biggest obstacles. By showing that any girl can do it, our girl authors are role models and inspirations for all girls.

TO ORDER OR TO REQUEST A CATALOG, CONTACT
Beyond Words Publishing, Inc.
20827 N.W. Cornell Road, Suite 500
Hillsboro, OR 97124-9808
503-531-8700 or 1-800-284-9673

You can also visit our Web site at www.beyondword.com
or e-mail us at info@beyondword.com.

Beyond Words Publishing, Inc.

MISSION STATEMENT:

Inspire to Integrity

OUR DECLARED VALUES:

We give to all of life as life has given us.

We honor all relationships.

Trust and stewardship are integral to fulfilling dreams.

Collaboration is essential to create miracles.

Creativity and aesthetics nourish the soul.

Unlimited thinking is fundamental.

Living your passion is vital.

Joy and humor open our hearts to growth.

It is important to remind ourselves of love.